TREASURY OF
Baking

CRESCENT BOOKS

Project Editor: Cindy Young
Project Art Director: Anita Gindele
Recipe development and testing by The Duncan Hines Kitchens.

This edition published by:
Crescent Books
Distributed by Outlet Book Company, Inc.
A Random House Company
225 Park Avenue South
New York, NY 10003

Library of Congress Catalog Card Number: 91-67667

ISBN: 0-517-05896-0

Pictured on the front cover (*clockwise from right*): Linzer Hearts (*page 104*), Chocolate
Strawberry Dream Torte (*page 136*) and Cappucino Bon Bons (*page 35*).

Pictured on the back cover (*clockwise from right*): Blueberry Angel Food Cake Roll (*page 50*),
Nutty Blueberry Muffins (*page 68*), Cappucino Bon Bons (*page 35*) and Linzer Hearts
(*page 104*).

First published in the United States.

Manufactured in U.S.A.

8   7   6   5   4   3   2   1

MICROWAVE COOKING
Microwave ovens vary in wattage and power output; cooking times given with microwave
directions in this cookbook may need to be adjusted.

Helping You Bake Your Best

Greetings!

Welcome to the wonderful world of baking with Duncan Hines®
cake, muffin, brownie and cookie mixes! We're delighted to bring
you this special collection featuring some of our most requested
and best recipes. You'll find an assortment to choose from,
whether you're looking for a weeknight dessert for the family,
breakfast muffins for a busy morning, cookies and brownies for a
bake sale or an elegant cake for special celebration times.

All of our recipes are created in the Duncan Hines® Test Kitchens
by experienced home economists. Before our recipes are
developed, a number of factors are considered. Our research with
consumers just like you provides helpful information about the
flavors you like, the ingredients you keep on your pantry shelves,
the appliances in your kitchen and the baking equipment you
have available for recipe preparation. We also take into account
the cost of the ingredients required for the recipes. And, we know
you have busy schedules and need recipes that fit into your
life-styles. So, we consider the amount of time for preparing,
baking, cooling and assembling our recipes. After all, one
of the advantages of baking with Duncan Hines® mixes is
their convenience, in addition to their excellent flavor and
consistent reliability.

Our professional home economists also evaluate the recipes for
taste and appearance. The finished products must not only be
eye-catching, but scrumptiously good too! We put the recipes
through their paces, making sure they are easy to remove from
the baking pan, frost, decorate, cut and serve. We test and retest
our recipes until every aspect is satisfactory. Our goal is for
each Duncan Hines® recipe to yield perfect, delectable results
every time.

After creating the recipes, we divide the method into steps to make it easier for you to follow during preparation. Baking times are given along with doneness tests or visual clues so you will know when your baked goods are just perfect. We have included tips with each recipe to provide you with ideas for flavor variations, storage, uses for leftovers or information on preparation techniques. Some recipes include diagrams for help in arranging special occasion cakes and the beautiful photographs provide inspiration for trying them.

Duncan Hines® is a name you can trust and we hope Duncan Hines® TREASURY OF BAKING will become a standard reference in your kitchen library. Fill your home with the tantalizing aromas of baking! You have our assurance that Duncan Hines® recipes and products will please you every time

Happy Baking!

Cindy Young
Duncan Hines® Home Economist

From left to right in the Duncan Hines® Kitchens: Dianne Scott, Sandy Kraus, Cindy Young and Judy Sullivan

Spring and Summer Sensations

STRAWBERRY SHORTCAKE

12 Servings

CAKE
 1 package Duncan Hines®
  Moist Deluxe French
  Vanilla Cake Mix
 3 eggs
 1¼ cups water
 ½ cup butter or margarine,
  softened

FILLING and TOPPING
 2 cups whipping cream,
  chilled
 ⅓ cup sugar
 ½ teaspoon vanilla extract
 1 quart fresh
  strawberries, rinsed,
  drained and sliced
  Mint leaves, for garnish

1. Preheat oven to 350°F. Grease two 9-inch round cake pans with butter or margarine. Sprinkle bottom and sides with granulated sugar.

2. **For cake,** combine cake mix, eggs, water and butter in large bowl. Beat at medium speed with electric mixer for 2 minutes. Pour into pans. Bake at 350°F for 30 to 35 minutes or until toothpick inserted in center comes out clean. Cool in pans 10 minutes. Invert onto cooling rack. Cool completely.

3. **For filling and topping,** beat whipping cream, sugar and vanilla extract until stiff in large bowl. Reserve ⅓ cup for garnish. Place one cake layer on serving plate. Spread with half the remaining whipped cream and sliced strawberries. Repeat with remaining layer and whipped cream. Garnish with reserved whipped cream and mint leaves. Refrigerate until ready to serve.

> **Tip:** Whipping cream doubles in volume when whipped. For best results, chill bowl and beaters.

Strawberry Shortcake

BANANA FUDGE MARBLE CAKE

12 Servings

CAKE
- 1 package Duncan Hines® DeLights Fudge Marble Cake Mix
- 2 eggs
- 1 cup ripe mashed banana
- ½ cup water

FROSTING
- 1 package (4-serving size) banana instant pudding and pie filling mix
- 2 envelopes whipped topping mix
- 1¼ cups milk
- 1 banana, sliced
- Lemon juice
- ½ cup frozen whipped topping, thawed

1. Preheat oven to 350°F. Grease and flour two 9-inch round cake pans.

2. **For cake,** combine cake mix, eggs, mashed banana and water in large bowl. Beat at medium speed with electric mixer for 2 minutes. Pour into pans. Bake and cool following package directions.

3. **For frosting,** combine pudding mix, whipped topping mix and milk in large bowl. Beat at high speed with electric mixer for 2 to 3 minutes or until light and fluffy. Fill and frost cake. Refrigerate for several hours before serving. Dip banana slices in lemon juice. Blot dry. Garnish with whipped topping and banana slices.

> **Tip:** Serve cake slices with 2 tablespoons Fudge Sauce (see page 26).

ZUCCHINI CAKE

12 to 16 Servings

- 1 package Duncan Hines® Moist Deluxe Butter Recipe Golden Cake Mix
- 3 eggs
- ½ cup butter or margarine, softened
- ½ cup water
- 1 teaspoon ground cinnamon
- 2 cups grated zucchini
- ½ cup chopped walnuts
- Confectioners sugar

1. Preheat oven to 375°F. Grease 13×9×2-inch pan.

2. Combine cake mix, eggs, butter, water and cinnamon in large bowl. Beat at low speed with electric mixer until moistened. Beat at medium speed for 4 minutes. Stir in zucchini. Pour into pan; sprinkle with walnuts. Bake at 375°F for 30 to 35 minutes or until toothpick inserted in center comes out clean.

3. To serve, dust with confectioners sugar. Serve warm or cool completely.

> **Tip:** For a quick glaze, combine 1 cup confectioners sugar with 1 to 2 tablespoons water. Stir until smooth.

Banana Fudge Marble Cake

LEMON BLUEBERRY POPPY SEED BREAD

1 Loaf (12 Slices)

BREAD
   **1 package Duncan Hines®
      Bakery Style
      Blueberry Muffin Mix**
   2 tablespoons poppy seed
   1 egg
   ¾ cup water
   **1 tablespoon grated lemon
      peel**

DRIZZLE
   ½ cup confectioners sugar
   1 tablespoon lemon juice

1. Preheat oven to 350°F. Grease and flour 8½×4½×2½-inch loaf pan.

2. Rinse blueberries from Mix with cold water and drain.

3. **For bread,** combine muffin mix and poppy seed in medium bowl. Break up any lumps. Add egg and water. Stir until moistened, about 50 strokes. Fold in blueberries and lemon peel. Pour into pan. Sprinkle with contents of topping packet from Mix. Bake at 350°F for 1 hour or until toothpick inserted in center comes out clean. Cool in pan 10 minutes. Loosen loaf from pan. Invert onto cooling rack. Turn right-side up. Cool completely.

4. **For drizzle,** combine confectioners sugar and lemon juice in small bowl. Stir until smooth. Drizzle over loaf.

Tip: To help keep topping intact when removing loaf from pan, place aluminum foil over top.

Lemon Blueberry Poppy Seed Bread

STRAWBERRY SPLENDOR
CREAM CHEESE PIES

16 Servings

CRUST
1 package Duncan Hines® Moist Deluxe Swiss Chocolate Cake Mix
¾ cup butter or margarine, softened

FILLING
2 quarts fresh strawberries, rinsed, hulled and halved
1 cup sugar
¼ cup cornstarch
¼ teaspoon salt
¾ cup cold water
4 packages (3 ounces each) cream cheese, softened
¼ cup Citrus Hill® Orange Juice
Whipped cream, for garnish
Mint leaves, for garnish (optional)

1. Preheat oven to 350°F. Grease two 9-inch pie pans.

2. **For crust,** place cake mix in large bowl. Cut in butter with pastry blender or 2 knives until mixture is crumbly. Put half the crumbs in each pan. Press up sides and on bottom of each pan. Bake at 350°F for 15 minutes. Cool.

3. **For filling,** reserve 4 cups strawberries. Crush remaining strawberries with fork. Set aside. Combine sugar, cornstarch and salt in heavy saucepan. Add cold water gradually, stirring until smooth. Add crushed strawberries. Cook on medium heat, stirring constantly, until mixture comes to a boil. Cook and stir 1 minute. Remove from heat. Cool.

4. Beat cream cheese until softened. Beat in orange juice until smooth. Spread over bottoms of baked pie shells. Arrange reserved strawberries over cheese layer. Pour cooled strawberry mixture over halved strawberries. Refrigerate until ready to serve. Top each slice with dollop of whipped cream. Garnish with mint leaves, if desired.

Tip: To quickly crush strawberries, use a potato masher.

Strawberry Splendor Cream Cheese Pie

PINEAPPLE ORANGE POUND CAKE

12 to 16 Servings

CAKE
  1 package Duncan Hines®
    Moist Deluxe
    Pineapple Supreme
    Cake Mix
  1 package (4-serving size)
    vanilla instant pudding
    and pie filling mix
  4 eggs
  1 cup Citrus Hill® Orange
    Juice
  ⅓ cup Crisco® Oil or
    Crisco® Puritan® Oil
  1 tablespoon grated
    orange peel

GLAZE
  ⅓ cup sugar
  ¼ cup Citrus Hill® Orange
    Juice

1. Preheat oven to 350°F. Grease and flour 10-inch Bundt® pan.

2. **For cake,** combine cake mix, pudding mix, eggs, 1 cup orange juice, oil and orange peel in large bowl. Beat at medium speed with electric mixer for 2 minutes. Pour into pan. Bake at 350°F for 50 to 60 minutes or until toothpick inserted in center comes out clean. Cool 25 minutes in pan. Invert onto serving plate.

3. **For glaze,** combine sugar and ¼ cup orange juice in small saucepan. Simmer 3 minutes. Brush warm glaze on cake.

Tip: Serve with peach ice cream.

STRAWBERRIES AND CREAM CHEESECAKE TARTS

24 Mini Cheesecakes

CRUST
  1 package Duncan Hines®
    Moist Deluxe
    Strawberry Supreme
    Cake Mix
  ¼ cup butter or margarine,
    melted

FILLING
  2 packages (8 ounces
    each) cream cheese,
    softened
  3 eggs
  ¾ cup sugar
  1 teaspoon vanilla extract

1. Preheat oven to 350°F. Place 2½-inch foil liners in 24 muffin cups.

2. **For crust,** combine cake mix and melted butter in large bowl. Beat at low speed with electric mixer for 1 minute. Divide mixture evenly in muffin cups. Level but do not press.

3. **For filling,** combine cream cheese, eggs, ¾ cup sugar and vanilla extract in medium bowl. Beat at medium speed with electric mixer until smooth. Spoon evenly into muffin cups. Bake at 350°F for 20 minutes or until mixture is set.

(continued)

TOPPING

1½ cups dairy sour cream
¼ cup sugar
12 fresh strawberries,
   halved

4. **For topping,** combine sour cream and ¼ cup sugar in small bowl. Spoon evenly over cheesecakes. Return to oven. Bake for 5 minutes longer. Cool completely.

5. Garnish each cheesecake with strawberry half. Refrigerate until ready to serve.

> **Tip:** If you use dark-colored muffin pans, reduce the oven temperature to 325°F to prevent over-baking the tarts.

"KEY" LIME DESSERT SQUARES

16 Servings

CRUST

½ cup chopped pecans
1 package Duncan Hines®
   Moist Deluxe White
   Cake Mix
½ cup butter or margarine,
   melted

FILLING

3 egg yolks
1 can (14 ounces)
   sweetened condensed
   milk
⅔ cup lime juice
1 drop green food coloring
   (optional)
1 container (8 ounces)
   frozen whipped
   topping, thawed
   Lime slices, for garnish
   (optional)

1. Preheat oven to 350°F.

2. **For crust,** spread pecans in shallow baking pan. Bake 5 minutes or until lightly browned. Combine pecans, cake mix and melted butter. Stir until crumbs form. Spread in bottom of ungreased 13×9×2-inch pan. Press lightly.

3. **For filling,** combine egg yolks, sweetened condensed milk, lime juice and food coloring, if desired, in medium bowl. Stir until well blended. Spread over crust. Bake at 350°F for 15 minutes or until set. Cool 15 minutes. Refrigerate until chilled, about 2 hours.

4. To serve, cut into squares. Top with dollops of whipped topping and lime slices, if desired.

> **Tip:** Leftover egg whites will keep refrigerated in airtight container for a few days.

FRUIT AND CREAM COOKIE TART

12 Servings

CRUST
1 package Duncan Hines®
    Golden Sugar
    Cookie Mix

FILLING
1 package (8 ounces)
    cream cheese, softened
⅓ cup sugar
½ teaspoon vanilla extract

TOPPING
Peach slices
Banana slices
Fresh blueberries
Grape halves
Kiwifruit slices
Fresh strawberry slices
½ cup apricot preserves,
    warmed and strained

1. Preheat oven to 350°F.

2. **For crust,** prepare cookie mix following package directions for original recipe. Spread evenly on ungreased 12-inch pizza pan. Bake at 350°F for 14 to 16 minutes or until edges are light brown. Cool completely.

3. **For filling,** combine cream cheese, sugar and vanilla extract in small bowl. Beat at low speed with electric mixer until smooth. Spread on cooled crust. Refrigerate until chilled.

4. **For topping,** dry fruits thoroughly. Arrange fruit in circles on chilled crust working from outside edge toward center. Brush fruit with warmed preserves to glaze. Refrigerate until ready to serve.

Tip: To keep bananas and peaches from turning brown, dip slices in lemon juice.

Fruit and Cream Cookie Tart

TWIN ANGEL FOOD PARTY PIES

12 to 16 Servings

1 package Duncan Hines® Angel Food Cake Mix

FILLING
2 packages (4-serving size each) chocolate instant pudding and pie filling mix
3 cups milk
½ teaspoon almond extract
1 container (16 ounces) frozen whipped topping, thawed and divided
1 can (21 ounces) cherry pie filling

1. Preheat oven to 375°F.

2. Prepare, bake and cool cake following package directions.

3. Cut cake in half horizontally with serrated knife. Place on serving plates with cut-sides up. Cut around cake 1½ inches from outer edge, down ¾ inch and through to center. Gently pull out cut cake to leave a 1½-inch-wide rim. Fill center hole with removed cake. Repeat for second half.

4. **For filling,** combine pudding mixes in large bowl. Prepare following package directions using 3 cups milk and ½ teaspoon almond extract. Fold in 2 cups whipped topping.

5. Fill each cake with half the pudding mixture. Spoon half the cherry pie filling around outer edge of each cake. Garnish each cake with dollops of remaining whipped topping. Refrigerate until ready to serve. To serve, cut cake into wedges.

Tip: Try different flavor combinations of instant pudding and pie filling such as vanilla instant pudding and pie filling mix and blueberry pie filling.

Twin Angel Food Party Pie

TROPICAL FRUIT DELIGHT

12 to 16 Servings

CAKE
1 package Duncan Hines®
   DeLights Lemon
   Cake Mix
½ cup Citrus Hill® Orange
   Juice
2 eggs
1 tablespoon grated
   orange peel
   Confectioners sugar

TOPPING
1 can (11 ounces)
   mandarin orange
   segments, undrained
1 can (8 ounces) crushed
   pineapple with juice,
   undrained
¼ cup granulated sugar
1 tablespoon cornstarch
1 tablespoon butter or
   margarine (optional)
1 banana, sliced
¼ cup flaked coconut
   (optional)

1. Preheat oven to 350°F. Grease and flour 10-inch Bundt® pan.

2. **For cake,** empty mix into large bowl. Add water to orange juice to equal 1⅓ cups. Add liquid, eggs and orange peel to mix. Beat at medium speed with electric mixer for 2 minutes. Bake and cool cake following package directions. Sift confectioners sugar over cooled cake.

3. **For topping,** drain mandarin oranges, reserving juice. Drain pineapple, reserving juice. Combine juices in 1-cup measure. Add water or orange juice to fruit juices to equal 1 cup. Pour into small saucepan. Combine granulated sugar and cornstarch. Stir into liquid. Cook on medium heat, stirring constantly, until thickened. Add butter, if desired. Stir until melted. Cool.

4. Stir mandarin oranges, pineapple and banana into cooled sauce. Cut cake into 16 servings. Spoon sauce over each serving. Sprinkle with coconut, if desired.

Tip: Sauce can be made ahead of time. Add fruits just before serving.

Tropical Fruit Delight

CHOCO-LEMON DELIGHT

12 to 16 Servings

**1 package Duncan Hines®
Moist Deluxe Devil's
Food Cake Mix**
FILLING
  1 cup granulated sugar
  3 tablespoons cornstarch
  ⅛ teaspoon salt
  1 cup water
  **2 egg yolks, slightly
    beaten**
  **1 teaspoon grated lemon
    peel**
  **2 tablespoons butter or
    margarine**
  **2 tablespoons lemon juice
    Confectioners sugar
    Frozen whipped
    topping, thawed, for
    garnish**

1. Preheat oven to 350°F. Grease and flour two 9-inch round cake pans.

2. Prepare, bake and cool cake following package directions for original recipe.

3. **For filling,** combine granulated sugar, cornstarch and salt in saucepan. Stir in water. Cook on medium heat, stirring constantly, until mixture comes to a full boil. Boil and stir 1 minute. Remove from heat. Gradually stir in egg yolks and lemon peel. Cook on medium heat until filling comes to a boil. Reduce heat to low. Cook 1 minute. Remove from heat. Add butter. Stir until melted. Stir in lemon juice. Refrigerate 1 hour.

4. To assemble, place one cake layer on serving plate. Spread with filling. Place second layer on top. Sift confectioners sugar over cake. Decorate with dollops of whipped topping around edge.

Tip: One small lemon will yield about 1 teaspoon grated peel and 2 tablespoons juice.

STRAWBERRY DELIGHT REFRIGERATOR CAKE

16 to 20 Servings

CAKE
  **1 package Duncan Hines®
    Moist Deluxe
    Strawberry Supreme
    Cake Mix**
  **2 packages (10 ounces
    each) sweetened,
    frozen sliced
    strawberries, thawed**

1. Preheat oven to 350°F. Grease and flour 13×9×2-inch pan.

2. **For cake,** prepare, bake and cool following package directions for original recipe. Poke holes 1 inch apart in top of cake using handle from wooden spoon. Puree thawed strawberries with juice in blender. Spoon evenly over top of cake allowing mixture to soak into holes.

(continued)

TOPPING

**1 package (4-serving size)
vanilla instant pudding
and pie filling mix**
1 cup milk
**1 cup whipping cream,
chilled**
**Fresh strawberries, for
garnish**

3. **For topping,** prepare pudding mix following package directions using 1 cup milk. Beat whipping cream in small bowl until stiff peaks form. Fold whipped cream into pudding mixture. Spread over cake. Garnish with fresh strawberries. Refrigerate at least 4 hours.

Tip: To spread whipped cream mixture easily, first drop by spoonfuls and then spread gently.

"IN THE PINK" CAKE

12 to 16 Servings

**1 quart vanilla ice cream,
softened**
**1 can (6 ounces) frozen
pink lemonade
concentrate, thawed
and divided**
Red food coloring
**1 package Duncan Hines®
Moist Deluxe Lemon
Supreme Cake Mix**
**1 cup whipping cream,
chilled**
**2 tablespoons
confectioners sugar**

1. Line bottom of 9-inch round cake pan with aluminum foil.

2. Combine ice cream, 1/3 cup lemonade concentrate and 5 to 6 drops food coloring. Stir until blended. Spread in pan. Freeze until firm. Run knife around edge of pan to loosen ice cream. Remove from pan. Wrap in foil and return to freezer.

3. Preheat oven to 350°F. Grease and flour two 9-inch round cake pans.

4. Prepare, bake and cool cake following package directions for original recipe.

5. To assemble, place one cake layer on serving plate. Place ice cream on cake. Peel off foil. Top with second cake layer. Place cake in freezer. Combine whipping cream, remaining lemonade concentrate, confectioners sugar and 2 or 3 drops food coloring in medium bowl. Beat until stiff. Frost cake. Return to freezer until ready to serve.

Tip: If only 12-ounce can of pink lemonade is available use 1/3 cup to blend into ice cream and 1/3 cup to mix with whipping cream. Use remaining concentrate to make lemonade using only 1½ cans of cold water.

12 to 16 Servings

1 package Duncan Hines®
  Moist Deluxe White
  Cake Mix

BUTTERCREAM ICING
½ cup Crisco® Shortening
½ cup butter or margarine,
  softened
1 teaspoon vanilla extract
4 cups sifted confectioners
  sugar
2 tablespoons milk
  Red food coloring
  Fresh flowers (tulips,
  daffodils, pansies), for
  garnish (see Tip)

1. Preheat oven to 350°F. Grease and flour two 9-inch oval or round cake pans.

2. Prepare, bake and cool cake following package directions for original recipe.

3. **For buttercream icing,** combine shortening and butter in large bowl. Beat at medium speed with electric mixer. Add vanilla extract. Add confectioners sugar gradually, 1 cup at a time, beating well on medium speed. Scrape sides and bottom of bowl often. Add milk. Beat at medium speed until light and fluffy. Tint icing pink with red food coloring. Reserve 1 cup frosting for decoration.

4. To assemble, place one cake layer on serving plate. Spread with pink icing. Top with second cake layer. Frost sides and top. Fill pastry bag with reserved frosting. Decorate cake using star tip and writing tip. Garnish with fresh flowers just before serving.

Tip: Be sure to use only non-toxic flowers. Rinse fresh flowers with cool water and dry with paper towels. Place small piece of plastic wrap under flowers that rest on cake.

Springtime Flower Cake

HOT FUDGE SUNDAE CAKE

12 to 16 Servings

1 package Duncan Hines®
  Moist Deluxe Dark
  Dutch Fudge
  Cake Mix
½ gallon brick vanilla ice
  cream

FUDGE SAUCE
1 can (12 ounces)
  evaporated milk
1¾ cups sugar
4 squares (1 ounce each)
  unsweetened chocolate
¼ cup butter or margarine
1½ teaspoons vanilla
  extract
¼ teaspoon salt
  Whipped cream, for
  garnish
  Maraschino cherries,
  for garnish
  Mint leaves, for garnish
  (optional)

1. Preheat oven to 350°F. Grease and flour 13×9×2-inch pan.

2. Prepare, bake and cool cake following package directions for original recipe.

3. Remove cake from pan. Split cake in half horizontally. Place bottom layer back in pan. Cut ice cream into even slices and place evenly over bottom cake layer (use all the ice cream). Place top cake layer over ice cream. Cover and freeze.

4. **For fudge sauce,** combine evaporated milk and sugar in medium saucepan. Stir constantly on medium heat until mixture comes to a rolling boil. Boil and stir for 1 minute. Add unsweetened chocolate and stir until melted. Beat over heat until smooth. Remove from heat. Stir in butter, vanilla extract and salt.

5. To serve, cut cake into serving squares. Spoon hot fudge sauce on top of each cake square. Garnish with whipped cream, maraschino cherries and mint leaves, if desired.

Tip: Fudge sauce may be prepared ahead and refrigerated in tightly sealed jar. Reheat when ready to serve.

Hot Fudge Sundae Cake

8 Servings

CRUST
**1 package Duncan Hines®
 Blueberry Muffin Mix,
 separated**
**¼ cup butter or margarine,
 softened**

FILLING
**1 quart vanilla ice cream,
 softened (see Tip)**
**½ cup crumb mixture,
 reserved from Crust**

TOPPING
**Can of blueberries from
 Mix**
**1 pint fresh strawberries,
 rinsed, drained and
 sliced**
**2 tablespoons sugar
 (optional)**

1. Preheat oven to 400°F. Grease 9-inch pie plate.

2. **For crust,** place muffin mix in medium bowl. Cut in butter with pastry blender or 2 knives. Spread evenly in ungreased 9-inch square baking pan. *Do not press.* Bake at 400°F for 10 to 12 minutes. Stir. Reserve ½ cup crumbs for filling. Press remaining crumbs against bottom and sides of pie plate to form crust. Cool completely.

3. **For filling,** spread ice cream over crust. Sprinkle with reserved crumbs. Freeze several hours or until firm.

4. **For topping,** rinse blueberries from Mix with cold water and drain. Combine strawberries and sugar, if desired.

5. To serve, let pie stand 5 minutes at room temperature. Top with blueberries and strawberries. Cut into 8 wedges using sharp knife.

Tip: Ice cream can be softened by allowing to stand at room temperature for 15 minutes or placed in the refrigerator for 30 minutes.

Patriotic Pie

CHERRY ANGEL DESSERT

16 Servings

1 package Duncan Hines®
    Angel Food Cake Mix
2 envelopes whipped
    topping mix
1 package (8 ounces)
    cream cheese, softened
    and cut into small
    pieces
1⅓ cups confectioners sugar
1 can (21 ounces) cherry
    pie filling

1. Preheat oven to 375°F.

2. Prepare, bake and cool cake following package directions.

3. Prepare whipped topping mix following package directions. Blend in cream cheese and confectioners sugar.

4. Trim crust from cake. Cut into bite-size pieces. Place half the cake pieces in ungreased 13×9×2-inch pan. Cover with half the cheese mixture. Repeat with remaining cake. Cover with remaining cheese mixture. Refrigerate several hours or overnight.

5. Spread pie filling over top of dessert. Refrigerate until ready to serve.

Tip: For a lower calorie dessert, use reduced calorie cream cheese and lite cherry pie filling.

CARROT CAKE

16 Servings

CAKE
1 package Duncan Hines®
    Moist Deluxe Yellow
    Cake Mix
2 cups grated fresh
    carrots
1 can (8 ounces) crushed
    pineapple with juice,
    undrained
½ cup water
3 eggs
½ cup Crisco® Oil or
    Crisco® Puritan® Oil
½ cup finely chopped
    pecans
2 teaspoons ground
    cinnamon

1. Preheat oven to 350°F. Grease and flour 13×9×2-inch pan.

2. **For cake,** combine cake mix, carrots, pineapple with juice, water, eggs, oil, pecans and cinnamon in large bowl. Beat at low speed with electric mixer until moistened. Beat at medium speed for 2 minutes. Pour into pan. Bake at 350°F for 35 to 40 minutes or until toothpick inserted in center comes out clean. Cool in pan.

(continued)

FROSTING

2 packages (3 ounces each) cream cheese, softened

⅓ cup butter or margarine, softened

1½ teaspoons vanilla extract

3½ cups confectioners sugar

1 teaspoon milk

3. **For frosting,** combine cream cheese, butter and vanilla extract in large bowl. Beat at medium speed with electric mixer until smooth. Gradually add confectioners sugar and milk, mixing well. Spread on cooled cake. Refrigerate until ready to serve.

> **Tip:** Score cake into serving pieces and decorate with pineapple tidbits and pecan halves.

DOUBLE ORANGE REFRIGERATOR CAKE

16 to 20 Servings

CAKE

1 package Duncan Hines® Moist Deluxe Orange Supreme Cake Mix

1 package (4-serving size) orange flavored gelatin

¾ cup boiling water

½ cup cold water

TOPPING

1 can (8 ounces) mandarin orange segments, drained

1 container (8 ounces) frozen whipped topping, thawed

1 package (4-serving size) vanilla instant pudding and pie filling mix

⅔ cup water

Additional mandarin orange segments, for garnish

1. Preheat oven to 350°F. Grease and flour 13×9×2-inch pan.

2. **For cake,** prepare and bake following package directions for original recipe. Cool 25 minutes. Dissolve gelatin in ¾ cup boiling water. Stir in ½ cup cold water. Set aside at room temperature. Stir occasionally. Poke holes in top of warm cake with toothpick or long-tined fork. Pour gelatin mixture slowly over cake. Refrigerate.

3. **For topping,** combine mandarin oranges, whipped topping, pudding mix and ⅔ cup water in large bowl. Stir until ingredients are well blended, crushing mandarin oranges slightly. Spread topping over cake. Garnish with additional mandarin oranges. Refrigerate until ready to serve.

> **Tip:** To prevent cakes from picking up other flavors in the refrigerator, cover with plastic wrap.

Perfectly Simple

PARTY SQUARES

16 Servings

**1 package Duncan Hines®
Moist Deluxe Swiss
Chocolate Cake Mix
1 container (16 ounces)
Duncan Hines®
Vanilla Layer Cake
Frosting, divided
Red food coloring
2 bars (1.55 ounces each)
milk chocolate**

1. Preheat oven to 350°F. Grease and flour 13×9×2-inch pan.

2. Prepare, bake and cool cake following package directions for original recipe.

3. Reserve ⅓ cup Vanilla frosting. Tint remaining Vanilla frosting pink with red food coloring. Frost cake with pink frosting. Using a spatula, make diagonal lines in frosting across top of cake. Mark 16 servings with tip of knife.

4. Score milk chocolate bars into sections. Place chocolate pieces on top of each serving. Place star tip in pastry bag; fill with reserved Vanilla frosting. Pipe star partially on each chocolate piece to anchor. Cut cake into servings following knife markings in frosting.

Tip: This simple cake has many decorating options. Try reserving ⅓ cup frosting and tinting with green food coloring. Leave remaining frosting white. Decorate as above except fit pastry bag with leaf tip.

Party Squares

CAPPUCINO BON BONS

40 Bon Bons

1 package Duncan Hines®
  Fudge Brownie Mix,
  Family Size
2 eggs
⅓ cup water
⅓ cup Crisco® Oil or
  Crisco® Puritan® Oil
1½ tablespoons Folgers®
  Coffee Crystals
1 teaspoon ground
  cinnamon
  Whipped topping, for
  garnish
  Ground cinnamon, for
  garnish

1. Preheat oven to 350°F. Place 40 (2-inch) foil liners on baking sheets.

2. Combine brownie mix, eggs, water, oil, coffee and 1 teaspoon cinnamon in large bowl. Stir with spoon until well blended, about 50 strokes. Fill each liner with 1 measuring tablespoonful batter. Bake at 350°F for 12 to 15 minutes or until toothpick inserted in center comes out clean. Cool completely. Garnish with whipped topping and a dash of cinnamon. Refrigerate until ready to serve.

> **Tip:** To make larger Bon Bons, use twelve 2½-inch foil liners and fill with ¼ cup batter. Bake for 28 to 30 minutes.

GERMAN CHOCOLATE BROWNIES

24 Brownies

1 package Duncan Hines®
  Brownies Plus Milk
  Chocolate Chunks
  Mix
2 eggs
⅓ cup water
⅓ cup Crisco® Oil or
  Crisco® Puritan® Oil
½ cup firmly packed brown
  sugar
2 tablespoons butter or
  margarine, softened
1 tablespoon all-purpose
  flour
½ cup chopped pecans
½ cup flaked coconut

1. Preheat oven to 350°F. Grease bottom of 13×9×2-inch pan.

2. Combine brownie mix, eggs, water and oil in large bowl. Stir with spoon until well blended, about 50 strokes. Spread in pan.

3. Combine brown sugar, butter and flour in small bowl. Mix until well blended. Stir in pecans and coconut. Sprinkle mixture over batter. Bake at 350°F for 25 to 30 minutes or until topping is browned. Cool completely. Cut into bars.

> **Tip:** Always mix brownies by hand. Never use electric mixer.

Cappucino Bon Bons

PRALINE BROWNIES

16 Brownies

BROWNIES
 1 package Duncan Hines®
   Brownies Plus Milk
   Chocolate Chunks
   Mix
 2 eggs
 ⅓ cup water
 ⅓ cup Crisco® Oil or
   Crisco® Puritan® Oil
 ¾ cup chopped pecans
TOPPING
 ¾ cup firmly packed brown
   sugar
 ¾ cup chopped pecans
 ¼ cup butter or margarine,
   melted
 2 tablespoons milk
 ½ teaspoon vanilla extract

1. Preheat oven to 350°F. Grease 9-inch square pan.

2. **For brownies,** combine brownie mix, eggs, water, oil and ¾ cup pecans in large bowl. Stir with spoon until well blended, about 50 strokes. Spread in pan. Bake at 350°F for 35 to 40 minutes. Remove from oven.

3. **For topping,** combine brown sugar, ¾ cup pecans, melted butter, milk and vanilla extract in small bowl. Stir with spoon until well blended. Spread over hot brownies. Return to oven. Bake for 15 minutes longer or until topping is set. Cool completely. Cut into bars.

Tip: To keep leftover pecans fresh, store in freezer in airtight container.

PEACH CHANTILLY

12 Servings

 1 package Duncan Hines®
   Moist Deluxe White
   Cake Mix
 2 containers (8 ounces
   each) peach yogurt
 1 cup frozen whipped
   topping, thawed
 2 peaches
   Ground nutmeg

1. Preheat oven to 350°F. Grease and flour 13×9×2-inch pan.

2. Prepare, bake and cool cake following package directions for original recipe.

3. Place yogurt in small bowl. Fold in whipped topping. Finely dice 1 peach; fold into topping. Cut second peach into 12 thin slices.

4. To serve, cut cake into 3-inch squares. Place on serving plates. Spoon peach topping on each serving; top with peach slice. Sprinkle with nutmeg.

Tip: You can use other yogurt flavors and fresh fruit in place of peach yogurt and peaches.

Praline Brownies

DUMP CAKE

12 to 16 Servings

1 can (20 ounces) crushed pineapple with juice, undrained
1 can (21 ounces) cherry pie filling
1 package Duncan Hines® Moist Deluxe Yellow Cake Mix
1 cup chopped pecans or walnuts
½ cup butter or margarine, cut into thin slices

1. Preheat oven to 350°F. Grease 13×9×2-inch pan.

2. Dump pineapple with juice into pan. Spread evenly. Dump in pie filling. Spread evenly. Sprinkle cake mix evenly over cherry layer. Sprinkle pecans over cake mix. Dot with butter. Bake at 350°F for 50 minutes or until top is lightly browned. Serve warm or at room temperature.

Tip: You can use Duncan Hines® Moist Deluxe Pineapple Supreme Cake Mix in place of Moist Deluxe Yellow Cake Mix.

TAKE-ALONG CAKE

12 to 16 Servings

1 package Duncan Hines® Moist Deluxe Swiss Chocolate Cake Mix
1 package (12 ounces) semi-sweet chocolate chips
1 cup miniature marshmallows
¼ cup butter or margarine, melted
½ cup firmly packed brown sugar
½ cup chopped pecans or walnuts

1. Preheat oven to 350°F. Grease and flour 13×9×2-inch pan.

2. Prepare cake following package directions for original recipe. Add chocolate chips and marshmallows to batter. Pour into pan. Drizzle melted butter over batter. Sprinkle with brown sugar and top with pecans. Bake at 350°F for 45 to 55 minutes. Serve warm or cool completely.

Tip: Chocolate should be stored in a cool, dry place. When the storage area becomes too warm, chocolate will develop a "bloom" or a visible gray coating. Bloom has no effect on either the flavor or the quality of the chocolate and you may still use the chocolate in baking with excellent results.

BROWNIE KISS CUPS

25 Brownie Cups

1 package Duncan Hines®
    Fudge Brownie Mix,
    Family Size
1 egg
⅓ cup water
⅓ cup Crisco® Oil or
    Crisco® Puritan® Oil
25 milk chocolate candy
    kisses, wrappers
    removed

1. Preheat oven to 350°F. Place 25 (2-inch) foil liners in muffin pans or on baking sheets.

2. Combine brownie mix, egg, water and oil in large bowl. Stir with spoon until well blended, about 50 strokes. Fill each liner with 2 measuring tablespoonfuls batter. Bake at 350°F for 17 to 20 minutes. Remove from oven. Place 1 milk chocolate candy kiss on each cupcake. Bake 1 minute longer. Cool 5 to 10 minutes in pans. Remove to cooling racks. Cool completely.

> **Tip:** Substitute milk chocolate stars in place of candy kisses.

PECAN DIPPED CHOCOLATE CAKE

16 to 20 Servings

1 package Duncan Hines®
    Moist Deluxe Devil's
    Food Cake Mix
1 container (16 ounces)
    Duncan Hines®
    Chocolate Layer Cake
    Frosting, divided
25 to 30 pecan halves

1. Preheat oven to 350°F. Grease and flour 13×9×2-inch pan.

2. Prepare, bake and cool cake following package directions for original recipe.

3. Measure ¼ cup Chocolate frosting into small microwave-safe measuring cup. Microwave at HIGH (100% power) for 15 seconds; stir until smooth. Dip bottom third of pecan halves in melted frosting. Place on waxed-paper-lined baking sheet. Refrigerate 10 minutes or until set. Stir melted frosting into remaining frosting in container.

4. Frost cake with Chocolate frosting. Arrange dipped pecans as desired.

> **Tip:** For uniformity, choose pecan halves that are all approximately the same size.

PECAN FUDGE SHEETCAKE

20 Servings

1 package Duncan Hines®
  Moist Deluxe Devil's
  Food Cake Mix
½ cup butter or margarine
¼ cup *plus* 2 tablespoons
  milk
¼ cup unsweetened cocoa
1 pound confectioners
  sugar (3½ to 4 cups)
1 teaspoon vanilla extract
¾ cup chopped pecans

1. Preheat oven to 350°F. Grease 15½×10½×1-inch pan.

2. Prepare cake following package directions for original recipe. Pour into pan. Bake at 350°F for 20 to 25 minutes or until toothpick inserted in center comes out clean.

3. For frosting, place butter, milk and cocoa in medium saucepan. Stir on low heat until butter is melted. Add confectioners sugar and vanilla extract, stirring until smooth. Stir in pecans. Pour over warm cake. Cool completely.

> **Tip:** For best results, allow the cake to cool undisturbed until frosting is set, about 4 hours.

MISSISSIPPI MUD BROWNIES

20 to 24 Brownies

1 package Duncan Hines®
  Fudge Brownie Mix,
  Family Size
2 eggs
⅓ cup water
⅓ cup Crisco® Oil or
  Crisco® Puritan® Oil
1 jar (7 ounces)
  marshmallow creme
1 container (16 ounces)
  Duncan Hines® Milk
  Chocolate Layer Cake
  Frosting, melted

1. Preheat oven to 350°F. Grease bottom of 13×9×2-inch pan.

2. Combine brownie mix, eggs, water and oil in large bowl. Stir with spoon until well blended, about 50 strokes. Spread in pan. Bake at 350°F for 25 to 28 minutes or until set.

3. Spread marshmallow creme gently over hot brownies. Pour 1¼ cups melted Milk Chocolate frosting over marshmallow creme. Swirl with knife to marble. Cool completely. Cut into bars.

Note: Store leftover melted frosting in original container. Refrigerate.

> **Tip:** For ease in spreading marshmallow creme, place spoonfuls evenly over brownie surface. Allow heat of brownies to soften marshmallow creme before spreading.

Pecan Fudge Sheetcake

BROWNIE CANDY CUPS

30 Brownie Cups

1 package Duncan Hines®
   Brownies Plus Double
   Fudge Mix
2 eggs
⅓ cup water
¼ cup Crisco® Oil or
   Crisco® Puritan® Oil
30 miniature peanut butter
   cup candies, wrappers
   removed

1. Preheat oven to 350°F. Place 30 (2-inch) foil liners in muffin pans or on baking sheets.

2. Combine brownie mix, contents of fudge packet from Mix, eggs, water and oil in large bowl. Stir with spoon until well blended, about 50 strokes. Fill each liner with 2 measuring tablespoonfuls batter. Bake at 350°F for 10 minutes. Remove from oven. Push 1 peanut butter cup candy in center of each cupcake until top is even with surface of brownie. Bake 5 to 7 minutes longer. Cool 5 to 10 minutes in pans. Remove to cooling racks. Cool completely.

> **Tip:** Pack these brownies in your child's lunch bag for a special treat.

COCONUT CHOCOLATE CHIP COOKIES

3 Dozen Cookies

1 package Duncan Hines®
   Chocolate Chip
   Cookie Mix
1 egg
2 teaspoons water
2 cups flaked coconut

1. Preheat oven to 375°F.

2. Combine cookie mix, contents of buttery flavor packet from Mix, egg and water in large bowl. Stir until thoroughly blended. Drop by rounded teaspoonfuls into coconut. Roll to cover. Place 2 inches apart on ungreased baking sheets. Bake at 375°F for 10 to 11 minutes or until light golden brown. Cool 1 minute on baking sheets. Remove to cooling racks. Cool completely. Store in airtight container.

> **Tip:** For easier blending of cookie ingredients, stir dry mix with a fork to break up any lumps before adding remaining ingredients.

Brownie Candy Cups

PECAN DATE BARS

32 Bars

CRUST
  **1 package Duncan Hines®
    Moist Deluxe White
    Cake Mix**
  **⅓ cup butter or margarine,
    softened**
  1 egg
TOPPING
  **1 package (8 ounces)
    chopped dates**
  1¼ cups chopped pecans
  1 cup water
  **½ teaspoon vanilla extract
    Confectioners sugar**

1. Preheat oven to 350°F. Grease and flour 13×9×2-inch pan.

2. **For crust,** place cake mix in large bowl. Cut in butter with pastry blender or 2 knives until mixture is crumbly. Add egg; stir well (mixture will be crumbly). Pat mixture into bottom of pan.

3. **For topping,** combine dates, pecans and water in medium saucepan. Bring to a boil. Reduce heat and simmer until mixture thickens, stirring constantly. Remove from heat. Stir in vanilla extract. Spread date mixture evenly over crust. Bake at 350°F for 25 to 30 minutes. Cool completely. Dust with confectioners sugar. Cut into bars.

Tip: Pecan Date Bars are moist and store well in airtight containers. Dust with confectioners sugar to freshen before serving.

PEANUTTY ORANGE CAKE

16 to 20 Servings

  **1 package Duncan Hines®
    Moist Deluxe Orange
    Supreme Cake Mix**
  **¾ cup firmly packed brown
    sugar**
  **⅔ cup Jif® Creamy Peanut
    Butter**
  ¼ cup butter or margarine
  ¼ cup milk
  ¾ cup chopped peanuts

1. Preheat oven to 350°F. Grease and flour 13×9×2-inch pan.

2. Prepare and bake cake following package directions for original recipe.

3. For topping, set oven to broil. Place brown sugar, peanut butter, butter and milk in medium saucepan. Stir on medium heat until warm and smooth. Remove from heat. Stir in peanuts. Spread topping over warm cake. Broil 3 inches from heat for 1 minute or until golden brown. Cool completely.

Tip: Also delicious using Duncan Hines® Moist Deluxe Banana Supreme Cake Mix.

Pecan Date Bars

EASY GERMAN
CHOCOLATE CAKE

12 to 16 Servings

CAKE
  **1 package Duncan Hines®
    Moist Deluxe Swiss
    Chocolate Cake Mix**
  3 eggs
  1¼ cups water
  **½ cup Crisco® Oil or
    Crisco® Puritan® Oil**
  ½ cup chopped pecans

TOPPING
  **1 cup firmly packed brown
    sugar**
  **⅓ cup butter or margarine,
    melted**
  ¼ cup milk
  **1 can (3½ ounces) flaked
    coconut**
  ½ cup chopped pecans

1. Preheat oven to 350°F. Grease and flour 13×9×2-inch pan.

2. **For cake,** combine cake mix, eggs, water and oil in large bowl. Beat at medium speed with electric mixer for 2 minutes. Stir in ½ cup pecans. Pour into pan. Bake at 350°F for 35 to 40 minutes or until toothpick inserted in center comes out clean. Cool completely.

3. **For topping,** set oven to broil. Combine brown sugar, melted butter and milk in large microwave-safe bowl. Microwave at HIGH (100% power) for 1 to 2 minutes or until mixture comes to a boil. Stir in coconut and ½ cup pecans. Spread evenly over cooled cake. Broil 4 inches from heat for 3 to 5 minutes or until golden brown. Cool completely. Garnish as desired.

Tip: Rotate cake under broiler for more even browning.

GOLDEN OATMEAL MUFFINS

2 Dozen Muffins

  **1 package Duncan Hines®
    Moist Deluxe Butter
    Recipe Golden
    Cake Mix**
  **1 cup quick-cooking oats
    (not instant or
    old-fashioned)**
  ¼ teaspoon salt
  ¾ cup milk
  2 eggs, slightly beaten
  **2 tablespoons butter or
    margarine, melted**

1. Preheat oven to 400°F. Grease 24 (2½-inch) muffin cups (or use paper liners).

2. Combine cake mix, oats and salt in large bowl. Add milk, eggs and melted butter; stir until moistened. Fill muffin cups two-thirds full. Bake at 400°F for 13 minutes or until golden brown. Cool in pan 5 to 10 minutes. Loosen carefully before removing from pan. Serve with honey or your favorite jam.

Tip: For a slight variation, try adding 1 teaspoon ground cinnamon with the dry ingredients.

Easy German Chocolate Cake

DOUBLE CHOCOLATE CREAM CAKE

16 to 20 Servings

1 package Duncan Hines®
  Moist Deluxe Butter
  Recipe Fudge
  Cake Mix
1 envelope whipped
  topping mix
½ cup chocolate syrup
  Maraschino cherries
  with stems, for garnish

1. Preheat oven to 375°F. Grease and flour 13×9×2-inch pan.

2. Prepare, bake and cool cake following package directions for original recipe.

3. Prepare whipped topping mix following package directions. Fold in chocolate syrup until blended. Refrigerate until ready to serve.

4. To serve, spoon chocolate cream topping over cake slices. Garnish with maraschino cherries.

Tip: For best consistency, chill chocolate syrup before using.

ORANGE CHESS BARS

24 Bars

CRUST
  1 package Duncan Hines®
    Moist Deluxe Orange
    Supreme Cake Mix
  ½ cup Crisco® Oil or
    Crisco® Puritan® Oil
  ⅓ cup chopped pecans
TOPPING
  1 pound confectioners
    sugar (3½ to 4 cups)
  1 package (8 ounces)
    cream cheese, softened
  2 eggs
  2 teaspoons grated orange
    peel

1. Preheat oven to 350°F. Grease 13×9×2-inch pan.

2. **For crust,** combine cake mix, oil and pecans in large bowl. Stir until blended (mixture will be crumbly). Press in bottom of pan.

3. **For topping,** combine confectioners sugar and cream cheese in large bowl. Beat at low speed with electric mixer until blended. Add eggs and orange peel. Beat at low speed until blended. Pour over crust. Bake at 350°F for 30 to 35 minutes or until topping is set. Cool. Refrigerate until ready to serve. Cut into bars.

Tip: Also delicious using Duncan Hines® Moist Deluxe Yellow Cake Mix. Orange peel may be omitted, if desired.

CHOCOLATE ORANGE DELIGHT

12 to 16 Servings

CAKE
  1 tablespoon grated
    orange peel
  1 package Duncan Hines®
    DeLights Devil's Food
    Cake Mix

TOPPING
  1 container (8 ounces)
    frozen whipped
    topping, thawed
  2 tablespoons Citrus
    Hill® Frozen Orange
    Juice concentrate,
    thawed
    Orange slices, for
    garnish

1. Preheat oven to 350°F. Grease and flour 13×9×2-inch pan.

2. **For cake,** add orange peel to mix. Prepare, bake and cool cake following package directions.

3. **For topping,** combine whipped topping and orange juice concentrate in medium bowl. Stir until blended. Spoon dollop of topping on each cake serving. Garnish with orange slices. Refrigerate leftover topping.

Tip: To make orange juice from remaining concentrate, measure remaining concentrate; add 3 times the amount of water to concentrate.

WHITE CHOCOLATE BROWNIES

48 Small or 24 Large Brownies

1 package Duncan Hines®
  Brownies Plus
  Milk Chocolate
  Chunks Mix
2 eggs
⅓ cup water
⅓ cup Crisco® Oil or
  Crisco® Puritan® Oil
¾ cup coarsely chopped
  white chocolate
¼ cup sliced natural
  almonds

1. Preheat oven to 350°F. Grease bottom of 13×9×2-inch pan.

2. Combine brownie mix, eggs, water and oil in large bowl. Stir with spoon until well blended, about 50 strokes. Stir in white chocolate. Spread in pan. Sprinkle top with almonds. Bake at 350°F for 25 to 28 minutes or until set. Cool completely. Cut into bars.

Tip: For decadent brownies, combine 2 ounces coarsely chopped white chocolate and 2 tablespoons Crisco® Shortening in small heavy saucepan. Melt over low heat, stirring constantly. Drizzle over cooled brownies.

Cholesterol-Free Desserts

BLUEBERRY ANGEL FOOD CAKE ROLLS

16 to 20 Servings

1 package Duncan Hines®
    Angel Food Cake Mix
Confectioners sugar
1 can (21 ounces)
    blueberry pie filling
Mint leaves, for garnish
    (optional)

1. Preheat oven to 350°F. Line two 15½×10½×1-inch jelly-roll pans with aluminum foil.

2. Prepare cake following package directions. Divide into pans. Spread evenly. Cut through batter with knife or spatula to remove large air bubbles. Bake at 350°F for 15 minutes or until set. Invert cakes at once onto clean, lint-free dishtowels dusted with confectioners sugar. Remove foil carefully. Starting at short end, roll up each cake with towel jelly-roll fashion. Cool completely.

3. Unroll cakes. Spread about 1 cup blueberry pie filling to within 1 inch of edges on each cake. Reroll and place seam-side down on serving plate. Dust with confectioners sugar. Garnish with mint leaves, if desired.

Tip: For a variation in flavor, substitute cherry pie filling for blueberry pie filling.

Blueberry Angel Food Cake Roll

DELLA ROBBIA CAKE

12 to 16 Servings

CAKE
 1 package Duncan Hines®
  Angel Food Cake Mix
1½ teaspoons grated lemon
  peel

GLAZE
 6 tablespoons sugar
1½ tablespoons cornstarch
 1 cup water
 1 tablespoon lemon juice
 ½ teaspoon vanilla extract
  Few drops red food
  coloring
 6 cling peach slices
 6 medium strawberries,
  sliced

1. Preheat oven to 375°F.

2. **For cake,** prepare following package directions adding lemon peel with Cake Flour Mixture (red "B" packet). Bake and cool following package directions.

3. **For glaze,** combine sugar, cornstarch and water in small saucepan. Cook on medium-high heat until mixture thickens and clears. Remove from heat. Stir in lemon juice, vanilla extract and red food coloring.

4. Alternate peach slices with strawberry slices around top of cooled cake. Pour glaze over fruit and top of cake. Refrigerate leftovers.

Tip: Use only metal or glass mixing bowls when preparing angel food cake mixes. Plastic or ceramic bowls can retain traces of grease which will prevent the egg whites from reaching full volume.

SPICY OATMEAL RAISIN COOKIES

4 Dozen Cookies

 1 package Duncan Hines®
  Moist Deluxe Spice
  Cake Mix
 4 egg whites
 1 cup quick-cooking oats
  (not instant or old-
  fashioned)
 ½ cup Crisco® Puritan®
  Oil
 ½ cup raisins

1. Preheat oven to 350°F. Grease baking sheets.

2. Combine cake mix, egg whites, oats and oil in large bowl. Beat at low speed with electric mixer until blended. Stir in raisins. Drop by rounded teaspoonfuls 2 inches apart onto baking sheets. Bake at 350°F for 7 to 9 minutes or until lightly browned. Cool 1 minute on baking sheets. Remove to cooling racks. Store in airtight container.

Tip: For a flavor variation, use other Duncan Hines® cake mix flavors in place of spice cake mix.

Della Robbia Cake

PEANUT BUTTER BARS

24 Bars

1 package Duncan Hines®
    Peanut Butter
    Cookie Mix
2 egg whites
½ cup chopped peanuts
1 cup confectioners sugar
2 tablespoons water
½ teaspoon vanilla extract

1. Preheat oven to 350°F.

2. Combine cookie mix, contents of peanut butter packet from Mix and egg whites in large bowl. Stir until thoroughly blended. Press in ungreased 13×9×2-inch pan. Sprinkle peanuts over dough. Press lightly. Bake at 350°F for 16 to 18 minutes or until golden brown. Cool completely.

3. Combine confectioners sugar, water and vanilla extract in small bowl. Stir until blended. Drizzle glaze over top. Cut into bars.

Tip: Bar cookies look best when cut neatly into uniform sizes. Measure with ruler using knife to mark surface. Cut with sharp knife.

PEPPERMINT MARBLE
ANGEL CAKE

12 to 16 Servings

CAKE
1 package Duncan Hines®
    Angel Food Cake Mix
1 teaspoon peppermint
    extract
6 drops red food coloring

GLAZE
1 cup confectioners sugar
2 tablespoons skim milk
¼ teaspoon peppermint
    extract
3 drops red food coloring
1 peppermint candy stick,
    crushed (optional)

1. Preheat oven to 375°F.

2. **For cake,** prepare following package directions. Stir 1 teaspoon peppermint extract into batter. Divide in half; tint half with 6 drops red food coloring. Spoon batter into ungreased 10-inch tube pan alternating colors to marble. Bake and cool cake following package directions. Brush loose crumbs from cake with paper towel.

3. **For glaze,** combine confectioners sugar, milk, ¼ teaspoon peppermint extract and 3 drops red food coloring in small bowl. Stir until smooth. Drizzle over cake. Sprinkle with crushed peppermint candy, if desired.

Tip: After filling with batter, rap pan on counter 1 or 2 times to help remove any trapped air bubbles.

Peanut Butter Bars

SPECIAL HONEYED FRUIT CAKE

12 to 16 Servings

CAKE
1 package Duncan Hines®
   Moist Deluxe Butter
   Recipe Golden
   Cake Mix
6 egg whites
⅔ cup water
½ cup margarine, melted
1 tablespoon molasses
1 cup chopped nuts
½ cup raisins

SYRUP
¼ cup Citrus Hill® Orange
   Juice
¼ cup honey
¼ cup granulated sugar
   Juice and grated peel
   from 1 lemon
¼ teaspoon ground
   cinnamon

GLAZE
¾ cup confectioners sugar
2 tablespoons skim milk
½ teaspoon brandy
   Candied cherry halves
   Pecan halves

1. Preheat oven to 375°F. Grease and flour 10-inch Bundt® pan.

2. **For cake,** combine cake mix, egg whites, water, melted margarine and molasses in large bowl. Beat at medium speed with electric mixer for 2 minutes. Fold in nuts and raisins. Pour into pan. Bake at 375°F for 35 to 40 minutes or until toothpick inserted in center comes out clean. Cool 10 minutes. Invert onto serving plate. Return cake to pan. Poke holes in cake 1-inch apart with skewer or long-tined fork.

3. **For syrup,** combine all syrup ingredients in small saucepan on medium heat. Simmer 10 minutes, stirring occasionally. Pour hot syrup evenly over cake in pan. Cool cake completely before inverting onto serving plate.

4. **For glaze,** combine confectioners sugar, milk and brandy in small bowl. Beat until smooth. Drizzle over cooled cake. Decorate with candied cherries and pecans.

> **Tip:** For variety, substitute currants or dates for raisins.

Special Honeyed Fruit Cake

ORANGE WAKE UP CAKE

12 to 16 Servings

CAKE
- 1 package Duncan Hines® Moist Deluxe Yellow Cake Mix
- 3 egg whites
- 1¼ cups water
- ⅓ cup Crisco® Puritan® Oil
- 1 tablespoon grated orange peel

TOPPING
- ½ cup chopped pecans
- ⅓ cup firmly packed brown sugar
- ¼ cup fine graham cracker crumbs
- 2 tablespoons margarine, melted
- 1 tablespoon grated orange peel
- 1½ teaspoons ground cinnamon

GLAZE
- 1 cup confectioners sugar
- 2 tablespoons Citrus Hill® Orange Juice

1. Preheat oven to 375°F. Grease and flour two 9-inch round cake pans.

2. **For cake,** combine cake mix, egg whites, water and oil in large bowl. Beat at medium speed with electric mixer for 2 minutes. Fold in 1 tablespoon orange peel. Pour into pans.

3. **For topping,** combine chopped pecans, brown sugar, graham cracker crumbs, melted margarine, 1 tablespoon orange peel and cinnamon in medium bowl. Stir until well blended. Sprinkle over batter in pans. Bake at 375°F for 25 to 30 minutes or until toothpick inserted in center comes out clean.

4. **For glaze,** combine confectioners sugar and orange juice in small bowl; mix until smooth. Immediately pour glaze over baked layers. Serve warm or at room temperature.

Tip: Recipe makes 2 cakes. If you like, serve one immediately and freeze the other for a quick coffeecake at a later time. Freeze in resealable plastic bag.

APRICOT DESSERT CAKE

16 to 20 Servings

CAKE
- 1 package Duncan Hines® Moist Deluxe White Cake Mix
- 3 egg whites
- 1¼ cups water
- ⅓ cup Crisco® Puritan® Oil
- ½ cup finely chopped dried apricots

1. Preheat oven to 350°F. Grease and flour 13×9×2-inch pan.

2. **For cake,** combine cake mix, egg whites, water and oil in large bowl. Beat at medium speed with electric mixer for 2 minutes. Fold in dried apricots. Pour into pan. Bake at 350°F for 30 to 35 minutes or until toothpick inserted in center comes out clean. Cool completely.

(continued)

APRICOT SAUCE
1 can (16 ounces)
unpeeled apricot
halves, drained
¼ cup superfine sugar
2 tablespoons lemon juice

3. **For apricot sauce,** place apricot halves, sugar and lemon juice in blender or food processor fitted with steel blade. Process until smooth. Pour sauce over cake slices to serve.

Tip: Use your food processor to quickly chop dried apricots. Combine ½ cup dry cake mix and apricots in work bowl fitted with the steel blade; process until finely chopped.

RASPBERRY SWIRL CAKE

12 to 16 Servings

1 package Duncan Hines®
Moist Deluxe French
Vanilla Cake Mix
RASPBERRY SAUCE
1 package (12 ounces)
frozen raspberries,
thawed
2 tablespoons seedless red
raspberry jam
1 tablespoon cornstarch
1 tablespoon water
1 container (16 ounces)
Duncan Hines® Cream
Cheese Layer Cake
Frosting

1. Preheat oven to 350°F. Grease and flour two 9-inch round cake pans.

2. Prepare, bake and cool cake following package directions for No Cholesterol recipe.

3. **For raspberry sauce,** place sieve over small saucepan. Push raspberries through sieve with spoon. Discard seeds. Add jam. Dissolve cornstarch in water in small cup. Add to saucepan. Cook on medium heat, stirring constantly, until sauce comes to a boil and thickens. Cool.

4. To assemble, place one cake layer (bottom-side up) on plate. Spread with raspberry sauce, reserving enough to drizzle on top. Place second layer on top. Frost sides and top of cake with Cream Cheese frosting. Drizzle with reserved sauce. Run knife through frosting and sauce to swirl.

Tip: You may use strawberries and strawberry jam in place of the raspberries and raspberry jam.

4 Mini-Loaves

**1 package Duncan Hines®
  Bakery Style
  Cinnamon Swirl
  Muffin Mix**
½ teaspoon baking powder
 2 egg whites
⅔ cup water
**½ cup chopped dried
  apricots**
½ cup chopped dates

1. Preheat oven to 350°F. Grease four 5⅜×2⅝×1⅞-inch mini-loaf pans.

2. Combine muffin mix and baking powder in large bowl. Break up any lumps. Add egg whites, water, apricots and dates. Stir until well blended, about 50 strokes.

3. Knead swirl packet from Mix for 10 seconds before opening. Cut off one end of swirl packet. Squeeze contents onto batter. Swirl into batter with knife or spatula, folding from bottom of bowl to get an even swirl. Do not completely mix into batter. Divide evenly into pans. Sprinkle with contents of topping packet from Mix.

4. Bake at 350°F for 30 to 35 minutes or until toothpick inserted in center comes out clean. Cool 15 minutes. Loosen loaves from pans. Lift out with knife. Cool completely. Garnish as desired.

Tip: This recipe may also be baked in greased 8½×4½×2½-inch loaf pan at 350°F for 55 to 60 minutes or until toothpick inserted in center comes out clean. Cool 10 minutes before removing loaf from pan.

Apricot Date Mini-Loaves

CHOLESTEROL-FREE DESSERTS 61

FANTASY ANGEL FOOD CAKE

16 Servings

1 package Duncan Hines®
   Angel Food Cake Mix
Red and green food
   coloring
1 container (16 ounces)
   Duncan Hines® Cream
   Cheese Layer Cake
   Frosting

1. Preheat oven to 375°F.

2. Prepare cake following package directions. Divide batter into thirds and place in 3 different bowls. Add a few drops red food coloring to one. Add a few drops green food coloring to another. Stir each until well blended. Leave the third one plain. Spoon pink batter into ungreased 10-inch tube pan. Cover with white batter and top with green batter. Bake and cool following package directions.

3. Follow directions on Cream Cheese frosting label for Cream Cheese Glaze. Glaze sides and top of cake. Divide remaining glaze in half and place in 2 different bowls. Add a few drops red food coloring to one. Add a few drops green food coloring to the other. Stir each until well blended. Using a teaspoon, drizzle green glaze around edge of cake so it will run down sides. Repeat with pink glaze.

Tip: For marble cake, run knife through batters.

Fantasy Angel Food Cake

SPICE CAKE WITH FRESH PEACH SAUCE

12 to 16 Servings

1 package Duncan Hines®
   Moist Deluxe Spice
   Cake Mix
SAUCE
   6 cups fresh sliced
      peaches
   1 cup water
   1/3 cup sugar
   1/8 teaspoon ground
      cinnamon

1. Preheat oven to 350°F. Grease and flour 10-inch Bundt® or tube pan.

2. Prepare, bake and cool cake following package directions for No Cholesterol recipe.

3. **For sauce,** combine peaches and water in large saucepan. Cook over medium heat 5 minutes. Reduce heat. Cover and simmer 10 minutes. Cool. Reserve 1/2 cup peach slices. Combine remaining peaches, sugar and cinnamon in blender or food processor. Process until smooth. Stir in reserved peach slices. To serve, spoon peach sauce over cake slices.

> **Tip:** Fresh peach sauce can be served either warm or chilled.

BLUEBERRY STREUSEL COFFEECAKE

16 to 20 Servings

1 package Duncan Hines®
   Moist Deluxe Yellow
   Cake Mix, divided
1 cup all-purpose flour
   Egg substitute equal
      to 2 eggs
2/3 cup warm water
1 package active dry yeast
1 can (21 ounces)
   blueberry pie filling
1/3 cup margarine, melted
2 tablespoons sugar

1. Preheat oven to 375°F. Grease 13×9×2-inch pan.

2. Combine 1 1/2 cups cake mix, flour, egg substitute, water and yeast in large bowl. Beat at medium speed with electric mixer for 2 minutes. Spread dough in pan. Spoon pie filling over dough. Combine remaining cake mix and melted margarine in medium bowl. Sprinkle over pie filling. Sprinkle with sugar. Bake at 375°F for 30 to 35 minutes or until golden brown. Serve warm.

> **Tip:** For a delicious flavor variation, try using cherry or peach pie filling.

Spice Cake with Fresh Peach Sauce

CHOCOLATY ORANGE CAKE

12 to 16 Servings

CAKE
  1 package Duncan Hines®
    Moist Deluxe Devil's
    Food Cake Mix
  Egg substitute equal
    to 3 eggs
  1⅓ cups Citrus Hill®
    Orange Juice
  ½ cup Crisco® Puritan®
    Oil
  1 teaspoon grated orange
    peel
GLAZE
  1 cup sifted confectioners
    sugar
  2 teaspoons margarine,
    softened
  1 teaspoon grated orange
    peel
  2 to 3 tablespoons Citrus
    Hill® Orange Juice

1. Preheat oven to 350°F. Grease and flour 10-inch Bundt® pan.

2. **For cake,** combine all cake ingredients in large bowl. Beat at medium speed with electric mixer for 2 minutes. Pour into pan. Bake at 350°F for 45 to 55 minutes or until toothpick inserted in center comes out clean. Cool in pan for 25 minutes. Invert onto serving plate. Cool completely.

3. **For glaze,** combine confectioners sugar, margarine and 1 teaspoon orange peel in small bowl. Add orange juice, 1 tablespoon at a time, until glaze is desired consistency. Spoon over cake.

> **Tip:** Use a clean toothbrush to remove excess orange peel from your grater.

NO-CHOLESTEROL PECAN DATE BARS

32 Bars

CRUST
  1 package Duncan Hines®
    Moist Deluxe White
    Cake Mix
  ⅓ cup margarine, softened
  1 egg white

1. Preheat oven to 350°F. Grease and flour 13×9×2-inch pan.

2. **For crust,** place cake mix in large bowl. Cut in margarine with pastry blender or 2 knives until mixture is crumbly. Add egg white; stir well (mixture will be crumbly). Pat into bottom of pan.

(continued)

TOPPING

1 package (8 ounces)
  pitted dates, chopped
1¼ cups chopped pecans
1 cup water
½ teaspoon vanilla extract
  Confectioners sugar

3. **For topping,** combine dates, pecans and water in medium saucepan. Bring to a boil. Reduce heat and simmer until mixture thickens, stirring constantly. Remove from heat. Stir in vanilla extract. Spread date mixture evenly over crust. Bake at 350°F for 25 to 30 minutes or until set. Cool completely. Dust with confectioners sugar. Cut into bars.

Tip: To save time, use 1 package (8 ounces) chopped, sugared dates in place of pitted dates.

L E M O N   A N G E L   F O O D   C A K E
W I T H   B L U E B E R R Y   S A U C E

12 to 16 Servings

CAKE

1 cup *plus* 3 tablespoons
  water
2 tablespoons lemon juice
  Few drops yellow food
  coloring
1 package Duncan Hines®
  Angel Food Cake Mix
1 teaspoon grated lemon
  peel

SAUCE

⅔ cup sugar
2 tablespoons cornstarch
⅛ teaspoon salt
⅔ cup water
2 cups frozen dry pack
  blueberries
  Additional grated lemon
  peel, for garnish

1. Preheat oven to 375°F.

2. **For cake,** combine 1 cup *plus* 3 tablespoons water, lemon juice and yellow food coloring in small bowl. Prepare cake following package directions *except* use water mixture for the 1⅓ cups water called for on the package. Add 1 teaspoon grated lemon peel and Cake Flour Mixture (red "B" packet). Bake and cool cake following package directions.

3. **For sauce,** combine sugar, cornstarch and salt in small saucepan. Stir in ⅔ cup water. Cook over medium heat, stirring constantly, until thickened. Remove from heat. Stir in frozen blueberries. Refrigerate until chilled.

4. Spoon chilled blueberry sauce on top of cake. If desired, reserve a small amount of sauce to spoon over individual cake slices. Garnish with additional grated lemon peel. Refrigerate until ready to serve.

Tip: For angel food cakes, always use a totally grease-free cake pan to get the best volume.

NUTTY BLUEBERRY MUFFINS

8 Large or 12 Medium Muffins

**1 package Duncan Hines®
Blueberry Muffin Mix**
2 egg whites
½ cup water
⅓ cup chopped pecans

1. Preheat oven to 400°F. Grease 2½-inch muffin cups (or use paper liners).

2. Rinse blueberries from Mix with cold water and drain.

3. Empty muffin mix into bowl. Break up any lumps. Add egg whites and water. Stir until moistened, about 50 strokes. Stir in pecans; fold in blueberries.

4. For large muffins, fill cups two-thirds full. Bake at 400°F for 17 to 22 minutes or until toothpick inserted in center comes out clean. (For medium muffins, fill cups half full. Bake at 400°F for 15 to 20 minutes.) Cool in pan 5 to 10 minutes. Loosen carefully before removing from pan.

Tip: To reheat leftover muffins, wrap muffins tightly in foil. Place in 400°F oven for 10 to 15 minutes.

ANGEL FOOD CAKE WITH APRICOT ORANGE SAUCE

16 to 20 Servings

**1 package Duncan Hines®
Angel Food Cake Mix**
SAUCE
1¼ cups apricot nectar
1 tablespoon cornstarch
**⅔ cup dried apricots,
chopped**
**1 can (11 ounces)
mandarin orange
segments, drained**

1. Preheat oven to 375°F.

2. Prepare, bake and cool cake following package directions.

3. **For sauce,** combine apricot nectar and cornstarch in small saucepan. Cook and stir on medium heat until mixture begins to thicken. Add apricots and mandarin oranges. Stir until blended, breaking up mandarin oranges. Remove from heat. Cool. To serve, spoon sauce over cake slices.

Tip: Sauce can be prepared ahead of time and stored in the refrigerator in tightly sealed container. Sauce will thicken when chilled. Let sauce stand at room temperature for 30 minutes, or warm slightly, before serving.

Nutty Blueberry Muffins

FUDGE CAKE WITH MELBA TOPPING

16 to 20 Servings

CAKE
1 package Duncan Hines®
  Moist Deluxe Dark
  Dutch Fudge
  Cake Mix
  Egg substitute equal
  to 3 eggs
1¼ cups water
½ cup Crisco® Puritan®
  Oil

RASPBERRY SAUCE
1 package (12 ounces)
  frozen dry pack
  raspberries, thawed,
  drained and juice
  reserved
½ cup sugar
2 teaspoons cornstarch
½ teaspoon grated lemon
  peel
1 can (29 ounces) sliced
  peaches in heavy
  syrup, drained

1. Preheat oven to 350°F. Grease and flour 13×9×2-inch pan.

2. **For cake,** combine cake mix, egg substitute, water and oil in large bowl. Beat at medium speed with electric mixer for 2 minutes. Pour into pan. Bake at 350°F for 35 to 40 minutes or until toothpick inserted in center comes out clean. Cool completely.

3. **For raspberry sauce,** combine reserved raspberry juice, sugar, cornstarch and lemon peel in medium saucepan. Bring to a boil. Reduce heat and cook until thickened, stirring constantly. Stir in raspberries. Cool.

4. Cut cake into serving squares. Place several peach slices on top of each cake square. Spoon raspberry sauce over peaches and cake. Serve immediately.

Tip: To separate juice from raspberries in one step, allow berries to thaw at room temperature in a tea strainer placed over a bowl.

Fudge Cake with Melba Topping

CHERRY ANGEL ROLLS

16 to 20 Servings

**1 package Duncan Hines®
Angel Food Cake Mix
Confectioners sugar
1 cup chopped maraschino
cherries, drained
½ cup flaked coconut
1 teaspoon maraschino
cherry juice
1 container (8 ounces)
frozen whipped
topping, thawed**

1. Preheat oven to 350°F. Line two 15½×10½×1-inch jelly-roll pans with aluminum foil.

2. Prepare cake following package directions. Divide into pans. Spread evenly. Cut through batter with knife or spatula to remove large air bubbles. Bake at 350°F for 15 minutes or until set. Invert cakes at once onto towels dusted with confectioners sugar (see Tip). Remove foil carefully. Starting at short end, roll up each cake with towel jelly-roll fashion. Cool completely.

3. Fold chopped cherries, coconut and cherry juice into whipped topping. Unroll cakes. Spread half of filling over each cake to edges. Reroll and place seam-side down on serving plate. Dust with confectioners sugar. Refrigerate until ready to serve.

Tip: Use clean, lint-free dishtowels to roll up cakes.

PUMPKIN CAKE

12 to 16 Servings

**1 package Duncan Hines®
Moist Deluxe Butter
Recipe Golden
Cake Mix
Egg substitute equal
to 3 eggs
1 cup water
1 cup solid pack pumpkin
1 teaspoon ground
cinnamon
¼ teaspoon ground ginger
¼ teaspoon ground nutmeg
1 cup chopped walnuts**

1. Preheat oven to 375°F. Grease and flour 13×9×2-inch pan.

2. Combine cake mix, egg substitute, water, pumpkin, cinnamon, ginger and nutmeg in large bowl. Beat at medium speed with electric mixer for 4 minutes. Stir in walnuts. Pour into pan. Bake at 375°F for 35 to 40 minutes or until toothpick inserted in center comes out clean. Cool completely (see Tip).

Tip: Dust with confectioners sugar.

Cherry Angel Roll

BLUEBERRY ORANGE LOAF

1 Loaf (12 Slices)

1 package Duncan Hines®
  Bakery Style
  Blueberry Muffin Mix
½ teaspoon baking powder
2 egg whites
⅔ cup Citrus Hill® Orange
  Juice
1 teaspoon grated orange
  peel

1. Preheat oven to 350°F. Grease 8½×4½×2½-inch or 9×5×3-inch loaf pan.

2. Rinse blueberries from Mix with cold water and drain.

3. Empty muffin mix into bowl. Add baking powder; stir to combine and break up any lumps. Add egg whites and orange juice. Stir until moistened, about 50 strokes. Fold in blueberries and orange peel. Pour into pan. Sprinkle contents of topping packet from Mix over batter. Bake at 350°F for 45 to 55 minutes or until toothpick inserted in center comes out clean. Cool in pan 10 minutes. Loosen loaf from pan. Invert onto cooling rack. Turn right-side up. Cool completely.

Tip: Freeze extra grated orange peel for future use.

AMARETTO APRICOT CAKE

12 to 16 Servings

1 package Duncan Hines®
  Moist Deluxe White
  Cake Mix
FILLING
1 jar (12 ounces) apricot
  preserves
2 tablespoons Amaretto
  liqueur

1. Preheat oven to 350°F. Grease and flour two 8-inch round cake pans.

2. Prepare, bake and cool cake following package directions for No Cholesterol recipe. Refrigerate layers for 1 hour. Cut each layer in half horizontally (see Tip on page 111).

3. **For filling,** combine preserves and Amaretto in small bowl; stir well.

4. To assemble, place one cake layer on serving plate. Spread with one-third filling. Repeat with remaining layers and filling, leaving top plain.

(continued)

TOPPING
   **3 cups frozen whipped
      topping, thawed
   Apricot halves
   Toasted slivered
      almonds (see Tip)**

5. **For topping,** frost sides and top with whipped topping. Garnish with apricot halves and almond slivers.

> **Tip:** To toast almonds, spread in a single layer on baking sheet. Bake at 325°F for 6 to 8 minutes or until fragrant and light golden brown.

CHOCOLATE CHERRY ANGEL FOOD CAKE

12 Servings

**½ cup finely chopped nuts
¼ cup finely chopped
   maraschino cherries,
   drained
¼ cup semi-sweet mini
   chocolate chips
 1 package Duncan Hines®
   Angel Food Cake Mix
½ cup Duncan Hines®
   Chocolate Frosting
   Additional maraschino
   cherries, for garnish
   Additional chopped
   nuts, for garnish**

1. Preheat oven to 375°F.

2. Combine ½ cup nuts, ¼ cup cherries, chocolate chips and Cake Flour Mixture (red "B" packet) in large bowl. Prepare, bake and cool cake following package directions.

3. Heat Chocolate frosting until thin. Glaze cake, allowing frosting to drizzle down sides. Garnish with additional cherries and nuts.

> **Tip:** After chopping maraschino cherries, allow them to drain on paper towels.

Family Favorites

A L M O N D   B U T T E R   L O A V E S

2 Loaves (16 Slices)

CRUST
½ cup firmly packed brown
   sugar
⅓ cup butter or margarine,
   softened
1 cup toasted almonds,
   finely chopped
   (see Tip)
½ cup all-purpose flour

CAKE
1 package Duncan Hines®
   Moist Deluxe Butter
   Recipe Golden
   Cake Mix
3 eggs
⅔ cup water
½ cup butter or margarine,
   softened

GLAZE
1 cup confectioners sugar
1 to 2 tablespoons water
¼ teaspoon almond extract
3 tablespoons sliced
   almonds, for garnish

1. Preheat oven to 350°F. Grease and flour two 9×5×3-inch loaf pans.

2. **For crust,** combine brown sugar and ⅓ cup butter in large bowl. Beat at medium speed with electric mixer until light and fluffy. Stir in toasted almonds and flour. Blend well. Divide and press evenly into pans.

3. **For cake,** combine cake mix, eggs, ⅔ cup water and ½ cup butter in large bowl. Beat at medium speed with electric mixer for 4 minutes. Pour into pans. Bake at 350°F for 45 to 50 minutes or until toothpick inserted in center comes out clean. Cool in pans 10 minutes. Invert onto cooling racks, crust-side up. Cool completely.

4. **For glaze,** combine confectioners sugar, 1 tablespoon water and almond extract in small bowl. Stir until smooth. Add water, 1 teaspoon at a time, until glaze is desired consistency. Spoon over cooled loaves. Sprinkle sliced almonds over top.

Note: For ease in slicing loaves, use a serrated knife.

Tip: To toast almonds, spread in a single layer on baking sheet. Bake at 325°F for 6 to 8 minutes or until fragrant and light golden brown. Cool before chopping.

Almond Butter Loaf

CHOCOLATE CHIP RASPBERRY JUMBLES

16 Bars

1 package Duncan Hines®
   Chocolate Chip
   Cookie Mix
½ cup seedless red
   raspberry jam

1. Preheat oven to 350°F.

2. Prepare chocolate chip cookie mix following package directions for original recipe. Reserve ½ cup dough.

3. Spread remaining dough into ungreased 9-inch square pan. Spread jam over base. Drop reserved dough by measuring teaspoonfuls randomly over jam. Bake at 350°F for 20 to 25 minutes or until golden brown. Cool completely. Cut into bars.

Tip: For delicious flavor variations, substitute strawberry or blackberry jam for the red raspberry jam.

CHOCOLATE ALMOND COCONUT BARS

24 Bars

1 package (6 ounces)
   slivered almonds,
   chopped
1 package Duncan Hines®
   Moist Deluxe Devil's
   Food Cake Mix
½ cup butter or margarine,
   melted
1½ cups flaked coconut,
   packed
3 eggs
1 cup semi-sweet mini
   chocolate chips

1. Preheat oven to 350°F. Toast almonds on baking sheet at 350°F about 5 minutes or until fragrant and light golden brown. Cool completely.

2. Combine cake mix, toasted almonds and melted butter in medium bowl. Press mixture into bottom of ungreased 13×9×2-inch pan.

3. Combine coconut and eggs in medium bowl. Stir with spoon until well blended. Spread over crust. Sprinkle with mini chocolate chips. Bake at 350°F for 20 to 25 minutes. Cool completely. Refrigerate until well chilled. Cut into bars.

Tip: For a frosted look, try spreading the chocolate chips while still warm.

Chocolate Chip Raspberry Jumbles

CHERRY CHOCOLATY CAKE

12 to 16 Servings

1 package Duncan Hines®
   Moist Deluxe Dark
   Dutch Fudge
   Cake Mix
1 package (8 ounces)
   cream cheese, softened
½ cup butter or margarine,
   softened
½ teaspoon almond extract
1 pound confectioners
   sugar (3½ to 4 cups)
1 cup frozen dark sweet
   cherries, thawed,
   chopped and well
   drained

1. Preheat oven to 350°F. Grease and flour two 9-inch round cake pans.

2. Prepare, bake and cool cake following package directions for original recipe.

3. Combine cream cheese, butter and almond extract in large bowl. Beat at medium speed with electric mixer until smooth. Gradually add confectioners sugar, mixing well after each addition. Measure ¾ cup cream cheese mixture. Place in small bowl; stir in cherries.

4. To assemble, place one cake layer on serving plate. Spread with cherry mixture. Place other layer on top. Frost sides and top with plain cream cheese frosting. Refrigerate until ready to serve.

Tip: You can use either fresh or canned dark sweet cherries.

RASPBERRY-GLAZED BROWNIES

24 Brownies

1 package Duncan Hines®
   Brownies Plus Milk
   Chocolate Chunks
   Mix
1 square (1 ounce)
   unsweetened chocolate,
   melted
2 tablespoons butter or
   margarine, softened
2 tablespoons light corn
   syrup
1 cup confectioners sugar
1 tablespoon milk
1 teaspoon vanilla extract
2 tablespoons seedless red
   raspberry jam

1. Preheat oven to 350°F. Grease and flour 13×9×2-inch pan.

2. Prepare, bake and cool brownies following package directions for original recipe.

3. Combine melted chocolate, butter and corn syrup in medium bowl. Stir in confectioners sugar, milk and vanilla extract. Add jam; mix well. Spread on top of cooled brownies. Cut into bars.

Tip: For a variation, replace jam with orange marmalade.

Cherry Chocolaty Cake

DOUBLE FUDGE
BROWNIE BARS

20 to 24 Bars

1 package Duncan Hines®
   Brownies Plus Double
   Fudge Mix
2 eggs
⅓ cup water
¼ cup Crisco® Oil or
   Crisco® Puritan® Oil
1 package (6 ounces)
   semi-sweet chocolate
   chips
1 cup peanut butter chips
½ cup chopped pecans
1 cup flaked coconut
1 can (14 ounces)
   sweetened condensed
   milk

1. Preheat oven to 350°F. Grease bottom of 13×9×2-inch pan.

2. Combine brownie mix, contents of fudge packet from Mix, eggs, water and oil in large bowl. Stir with spoon until well blended, about 50 strokes. Spread in pan. Bake at 350°F for 18 minutes. Remove from oven. Sprinkle chocolate chips over brownie base, then sprinkle with peanut butter chips, pecans and coconut. Pour sweetened condensed milk over top. Bake for 22 to 25 minutes longer or until light golden brown. Cool completely. Cut into bars.

Tip: For a delicious flavor variation, substitute butterscotch flavored chips for peanut butter chips.

CHOCOLATE CHIP
LAYER CAKE

12 to 16 Servings

1 package Duncan Hines®
   Moist Deluxe Yellow
   Cake Mix
1 package (4-serving size)
   vanilla instant pudding
   and pie filling mix
4 eggs
1 cup dairy sour cream
½ cup Crisco® Oil or
   Crisco® Puritan® Oil
1 package (6 ounces)
   semi-sweet chocolate
   chips
1 square (1 ounce)
   unsweetened chocolate,
   grated
½ cup chopped pecans

1. Preheat oven to 350°F. Grease and flour three 9-inch round cake pans.

2. For cake, combine cake mix, pudding mix, eggs, sour cream and oil. Beat at medium speed with electric mixer for 2 minutes. Stir in chocolate chips, grated chocolate and chopped pecans. Divide into pans. Bake at 350°F for 35 to 40 minutes or until toothpick inserted in center comes out clean. Cool in pans 15 minutes. Remove from pans; cool completely.

(continued)

2 cups frozen whipped
   topping, thawed and
   divided
1 container (16 ounces)
   Duncan Hines®
   Chocolate Layer Cake
   Frosting
   Pecan halves, for
   garnish (optional)

3. To assemble, place one cake layer on serving plate. Spread 1 cup whipped topping over cake. Repeat with remaining layers and whipped topping, leaving top plain. Frost sides and top with Chocolate frosting. Garnish with pecans halves, if desired. Refrigerate until ready to serve.

Tip: You can bake this cake in a greased and floured 10-inch Bundt® pan or tube pan for 50 to 60 minutes or until toothpick inserted in center comes out clean. Omit whipped topping, Chocolate frosting and pecan halves; dust with confectioners sugar when cooled.

BLUEBERRY SOUR CREAM COFFEECAKE

9 Servings

COFFEECAKE
 1 package Duncan Hines®
   Blueberry Muffin Mix
 ⅓ cup dairy sour cream
 ¼ cup milk
 1 egg
 ¼ cup blueberry preserves
GLAZE
 ½ cup confectioners sugar
2½ teaspoons water

1. Preheat oven to 375°F. Grease 8- or 9-inch round cake or pie pan.

2. Rinse blueberries from Mix with cold water and drain.

3. **For coffeecake,** combine muffin mix, sour cream, milk and egg in medium bowl. Stir until ingredients are moistened. Spread half the batter in pan.

4. Combine blueberries and preserves in small bowl. Spread half the blueberry mixture on top of batter. Spread remaining batter over blueberry layer. Spread remaining blueberry mixture on top, avoiding edges. Bake at 375°F for 30 to 35 minutes for 8-inch pan (25 to 30 minutes for 9-inch pan) or until golden.

5. **For glaze,** combine confectioners sugar and water in small bowl; stir until smooth. Drizzle over hot coffeecake. Serve warm.

Tip: Every time you open the oven door, the temperature will drop 25 to 30°F. Bake minimum time before checking for doneness.

BERRY FILLED MUFFINS

8 Muffins

1 package Duncan Hines®
    Blueberry Muffin Mix
1 egg
½ cup water
¼ cup strawberry jam
2 tablespoons sliced
    natural almonds

1. Preheat oven to 400°F. Place 2½-inch paper or foil liners in 8 muffin cups.

2. Rinse blueberries from Mix with cold water and drain.

3. Empty muffin mix into bowl. Break up any lumps. Add egg and water. Stir until moistened, about 50 strokes. Fill cups half full with batter.

4. Fold blueberries into jam. Spoon on top of batter in each cup. Spread gently. Cover with remaining batter. Sprinkle with almonds. Bake at 400°F for 17 to 20 minutes or until set and golden brown. Cool in pan 5 to 10 minutes. Loosen carefully before removing from pan.

> **Tip:** For delicious flavor variations, try substituting blackberry or red raspberry jam for the strawberry jam.

CHOCOLATE CARAMEL BARS

20 to 24 Bars

1 package Duncan Hines®
    Moist Deluxe Swiss
    Chocolate Cake Mix
1 package (14 ounces)
    caramels, unwrapped
¾ cup butter or margarine
1 can (5 ounces)
    evaporated milk
1 cup chopped pecans
1 package (6 ounces)
    semi-sweet chocolate
    chips

1. Preheat oven to 350°F. Grease and flour 13×9×2-inch pan.

2. Prepare cake mix following package directions for original recipe. Pour half of batter into pan. Bake at 350°F for 15 minutes.

3. Place caramels, butter and evaporated milk in small saucepan. Cook on low heat until caramels are melted. Stir in pecans. Pour over hot baked layer. Sprinkle with chocolate chips. Spread remaining cake batter over top. Bake at 350°F for 35 to 45 minutes. Cool completely. Cut into bars.

> **Tip:** Cake will not test done with toothpick. Bake until top looks dry or press cake gently with your fingertip. Cake is done if it springs back.

Berry Filled Muffins

DOUBLE NUT CHOCOLATE CHIP COOKIES

3 to 3½ Dozen Cookies

1 package Duncan Hines®
  Moist Deluxe Yellow
  Cake Mix
½ cup butter or margarine,
  melted
1 egg
1 package (6 ounces)
  semi-sweet chocolate
  chips
½ cup finely chopped
  pecans
1 cup sliced almonds,
  divided

1. Preheat oven to 375°F. Grease baking sheets.

2. Combine cake mix, melted butter and egg in large bowl. Beat at low speed with electric mixer until just blended. Stir in chocolate chips, pecans and ¼ cup almonds. Shape rounded tablespoonfuls dough into balls. Place remaining ¾ cup almonds in shallow bowl. Press top of cookie in almonds. Place 2 inches apart on baking sheets. Bake at 375°F for 9 to 11 minutes or until lightly browned. Cool 2 minutes on baking sheets. Remove to cooling racks. Cool completely. Store in airtight container.

Tip: To prevent cookies from spreading too much, allow baking sheet to cool completely before baking each batch of cookies.

TRIPLE CHOCOLATE COOKIES

3½ to 4 Dozen Cookies

1 package Duncan Hines®
  Moist Deluxe Swiss
  Chocolate Cake Mix
½ cup butter or margarine,
  melted
1 egg
½ cup semi-sweet
  chocolate chips
½ cup milk chocolate chips
½ cup coarsely chopped
  white chocolate
½ cup chopped pecans

1. Preheat oven to 375°F.

2. Combine cake mix, melted butter and egg in large bowl. Stir in remaining ingredients.

3. Drop by rounded tablespoonfuls 2 inches apart onto ungreased baking sheets. Bake at 375°F for 9 to 11 minutes. Cool 1 minute on baking sheets. Remove to cooling racks. Cool completely. Store in airtight container.

Tip: For longer storage, store cookies in an airtight container in freezer for up to 6 months.

Double Nut Chocolate Chip Cookies

SOCK-IT-TO-ME CAKE

12 to 16 Servings

STREUSEL FILLING
- 1 package Duncan Hines® Moist Deluxe Butter Recipe Golden Cake Mix, divided
- 2 tablespoons brown sugar
- 2 teaspoons ground cinnamon
- 1 cup finely chopped pecans

CAKE
- 4 eggs
- 1 cup dairy sour cream
- ⅓ cup Crisco® Oil or Crisco® Puritan® Oil
- ¼ cup water
- ¼ cup granulated sugar

GLAZE
- 1 cup confectioners sugar
- 1 tablespoon milk

1. Preheat oven to 375°F. Grease and flour 10-inch tube pan.

2. **For streusel filling,** combine 2 tablespoons cake mix, brown sugar and cinnamon in medium bowl. Stir in pecans. Set aside.

3. **For cake,** combine remaining cake mix, eggs, sour cream, oil, water and granulated sugar in large bowl. Beat at medium speed with electric mixer for 2 minutes. Pour two-thirds of batter into pan. Sprinkle with streusel filling. Spoon remaining batter evenly over filling. Bake at 375°F for 45 to 55 minutes or until toothpick inserted in center comes out clean. Cool in pan 25 minutes. Invert onto serving plate. Cool completely.

4. **For glaze,** combine confectioners sugar and milk in small bowl. Stir until smooth. Add more milk to thin glaze as needed. Drizzle over cake.

> **Tip:** For a quick glaze, heat ½ cup Duncan Hines® Vanilla Frosting in small saucepan over medium heat, stirring constantly, until thin.

Sock-It-To-Me Cake

JAMAICAN BANANA CAKE

16 to 20 Servings

CAKE
1 package Duncan Hines®
   Moist Deluxe Banana
   Supreme Cake Mix
½ cup finely chopped
   walnuts

TOPPING
¾ cup firmly packed brown
   sugar
⅓ cup Butter Flavor
   Crisco®
2 tablespoons milk
1 cup flaked coconut
⅓ cup chopped walnuts

1. Preheat oven to 350°F. Grease and flour 13×9×2-inch pan.

2. **For cake,** prepare following package directions for original recipe. Stir in ½ cup finely chopped walnuts. Pour into pan. Bake at 350°F for 33 to 38 minutes or until toothpick inserted in center comes out clean.

3. **For topping,** set oven to broil. Combine brown sugar, Butter Flavor Crisco® and milk in small saucepan. Cook on medium heat, stirring constantly for 2 minutes, or until shortening melts. Stir in coconut and ⅓ cup walnuts. Spread over warm cake. Broil 4 inches from heat for 2 to 3 minutes or until golden. Cool completely.

Tip: Rotate cake under broiler for more even browning.

CHOCOLATE CHIP CRISPERS

3 Dozen Cookies

1 package Duncan Hines®
   Chocolate Chip
   Cookie Mix
1 egg
1 tablespoon water
3 cups cocoa- or fruit-
   flavored crisp rice
   cereal

1. Preheat oven to 375°F.

2. Combine cookie mix, contents of buttery flavor packet from Mix, egg and water in large bowl. Stir until thoroughly blended. Shape dough into 36 (1-inch) balls. Place cereal in large resealable plastic bag. Seal bag and crush cereal with rolling pin. Drop several dough balls at a time into bag and shake until well coated. Place balls 2 inches apart on ungreased baking sheets. Bake at 375°F for 8 to 9 minutes or until light golden brown. Cool 1 minute on baking sheets. Remove to cooling racks. Cool completely. Store in airtight container.

Tip: For easier blending of cookie ingredients, stir cookie mix with fork to break up any lumps before adding remaining ingredients.

PINEAPPLE UPSIDE DOWN CAKE

16 to 20 Servings

TOPPING
½ cup butter or margarine
1 cup firmly packed brown
   sugar
1 can (20 ounces)
   pineapple slices, well
   drained
   Maraschino cherries,
   halved and drained
   Walnut halves

CAKE
1 package Duncan Hines®
   Moist Deluxe
   Pineapple Supreme
   Cake Mix
1 package (4-serving size)
   vanilla instant pudding
   and pie filling mix
4 eggs
1 cup water
½ cup Crisco® Oil or
   Crisco® Puritan® Oil

1. Preheat oven to 350°F.

2. **For topping,** melt butter on low heat in 12-inch cast-iron skillet or skillet with ovenproof handle. Remove from heat. Stir in brown sugar. Spread to cover bottom of skillet. Arrange pineapple slices, maraschino cherries and walnut halves in skillet. Set aside.

3. **For cake,** combine cake mix, pudding mix, eggs, water and oil in large bowl. Beat at medium speed with electric mixer for 2 minutes. Pour batter evenly over fruit in skillet. Bake at 350°F for 1 hour or until toothpick inserted in center comes out clean. Invert onto serving plate. Cut into wedges.

> **Tips:** Cake can also be made in a 13×9×2-inch pan. Bake at 350°F for 45 to 55 minutes or until toothpick inserted in center comes out clean. Cake is also delicious using Duncan Hines® Moist Deluxe Yellow Cake Mix.

48 Bars

CRUST
  ¾ **cup butter or margarine,**
    softened
  ¾ **cup firmly packed brown**
    sugar
  1 **egg yolk**
  ¾ **teaspoon vanilla extract**
  1½ **cups all-purpose flour**

FILLING
  1 **package Duncan Hines®**
    Fudge Brownie Mix,
    Family Size
  1 **egg**
  ⅓ **cup water**
  ⅓ **cup Crisco® Oil or**
    Crisco® Puritan® Oil

TOPPING
  1 **package (12 ounces)**
    milk chocolate chips,
    melted
  ¾ **cup finely chopped**
    pecans

1. Preheat oven to 350°F. Grease 15½×10½×1-inch pan.

2. **For crust,** combine butter, brown sugar, egg yolk and vanilla extract in large bowl. Stir in flour. Spread in pan. Bake at 350°F for 15 minutes or until golden.

3. **For filling,** combine brownie mix, egg, water and oil. Stir with spoon until well blended, about 50 strokes. Spread over hot crust. Bake at 350°F for 15 minutes or until surface appears set. Cool 30 minutes.

4. **For topping,** spread melted chocolate on top of brownie layer; sprinkle with pecans. Cool completely. Cut into bars.

Tip: Bars may be made ahead and frozen in an airtight container for several weeks.

Toffee Brownie Bars

CHERRY CAKE COBBLER

12 to 16 Servings

1 package Duncan Hines®
   Moist Deluxe French
   Vanilla Cake Mix
3 eggs
1⅓ cups water
⅓ cup Crisco® Oil or
   Crisco® Puritan® Oil
1 cup sugar
2 tablespoons cornstarch
2 cans (16 ounces each)
   pitted red tart cherries,
   undrained
2 tablespoons butter or
   margarine, melted
   Red food coloring
¾ teaspoon almond extract
   Whipped cream

1. Preheat oven to 350°F. Grease and flour 13×9×2-inch pan.

2. Combine cake mix, eggs, water and oil in large bowl. Beat at medium speed with electric mixer for 2 minutes. Pour into pan.

3. Combine sugar and cornstarch in large bowl. Add cherries with juice, melted butter, 8 to 12 drops food coloring and almond extract. Stir until blended. Spoon cherry mixture over batter. Bake at 350°F for 60 to 65 minutes or until golden. Serve warm or cold with whipped cream.

Tip: Also delicious using Duncan Hines® Moist Deluxe White Cake Mix.

CHOCOLATE OAT CHEWIES

4½ Dozen Cookies

1 package Duncan Hines®
   Moist Deluxe Devil's
   Food Cake Mix
1⅓ cups old-fashioned oats
   (not instant or quick-
   cooking)
1 cup flaked coconut,
   toasted and divided
   (see Tip)
¾ cup butter or margarine,
   melted
2 eggs, beaten
1 teaspoon vanilla extract
5 bars (1.55 ounces each)
   milk chocolate, cut into
   rectangles

1. Preheat oven to 350°F.

2. Combine cake mix, oats, ½ cup coconut, melted butter, eggs and vanilla extract in large bowl. Stir until blended. Cover and chill 15 minutes.

3. Shape dough into 54 (1-inch) balls. Place balls 2 inches apart on ungreased baking sheets. Bake at 350°F for 12 minutes or until tops are slightly cracked. Remove from oven. Press one milk chocolate rectangle into center of each cookie. Sprinkle with remaining ½ cup coconut. Remove to cooling racks. Cool completely. Store between layers of waxed paper in airtight container.

Tip: To toast coconut, spread on baking sheet and bake at 350°F for 3 minutes. Stir and bake 1 to 2 minutes longer or until light golden brown.

Cherry Cake Cobbler

ORANGE CINNAMON TEA CAKE

12 to 16 Servings

CAKE
- **1 package Duncan Hines® Moist Deluxe Orange Supreme Cake Mix**
- **3 eggs**
- **1⅓ cups Citrus Hill® Orange Juice**
- **⅓ cup Crisco® Oil or Crisco® Puritan® Oil**
- **1 teaspoon ground cinnamon**
- **½ cup chopped walnuts**

GLAZE
- **½ cup Duncan Hines® Vanilla Frosting**
- **1 tablespoon Citrus Hill® Orange Juice**
- **¼ cup chopped walnuts**

1. Preheat oven to 350°F. Grease and flour 10-inch Bundt® or tube pan.

2. **For cake,** combine cake mix, eggs, 1⅓ cups orange juice, oil and cinnamon in large bowl. Beat at medium speed with electric mixer for 2 minutes. Stir in ½ cup walnuts. Pour into pan. Bake at 350°F for 40 to 50 minutes or until toothpick inserted in center comes out clean. Cool in pan 25 minutes. Invert onto serving plate. Cool completely.

3. **For glaze,** combine Vanilla frosting and 1 tablespoon orange juice in small bowl. Stir until smooth. Drizzle over cake. Sprinkle with ¼ cup walnuts.

> **Tip:** Cake may be baked, wrapped and frozen for up to 6 weeks before using. Thaw unwrapped at room temperature.

CHOCOLATE ALMOND CRUNCH CAKE

12 Servings

CAKE
- **1¼ cups natural chopped almonds, divided**
- **1 package Duncan Hines® Moist Deluxe Swiss Chocolate Cake Mix**
- **3 eggs**
- **1¼ cups water**
- **½ cup flaked coconut**
- **½ cup Crisco® Oil or Crisco® Puritan® Oil**
- **2 bars (1.55 ounces each) milk chocolate, melted**

1. Preheat oven to 350°F. Grease and flour two 9-inch round cake pans.

2. Toast almonds in 350°F oven on baking sheet for 6 to 8 minutes or until fragrant and light golden brown. Cool completely.

3. **For cake,** combine cake mix, ½ cup toasted almonds, eggs, water, ½ cup coconut, oil and 2 melted chocolate bars in large bowl. Beat at medium speed with electric mixer for 2 minutes. Pour into pans. Bake and cool cake following package directions.

(continued)

FROSTING
   **1 cup butter or margarine,
      chilled and cut into
      pieces**
   **1 cup confectioners sugar,
      sifted**
   **4 bars (1.55 ounces each)
      milk chocolate, melted**
   ¼ cup flaked coconut

4. **For frosting,** combine butter, confectioners sugar and 4 melted chocolate bars in medium bowl. Beat at high speed with electric mixer for 3 minutes. Place one cake layer on serving plate. Spread with 1 cup frosting. Sprinkle with ½ cup toasted almonds. Top with second cake layer. Frost sides and top with remaining frosting. Garnish with ¼ cup coconut and remaining ¼ cup toasted almonds. Refrigerate until chilled.

Tip: The frosting becomes firm when chilled. To cut cake easily, let cake stand 1 hour at room temperature before serving.

FRENCH VANILLA BRICKLE CAKE

12 to 16 Servings

CAKE
   **1 package Duncan Hines®
      Moist Deluxe French
      Vanilla Cake Mix**
   **1 package (4-serving size)
      vanilla instant pudding
      and pie filling mix**
   4 eggs
   **½ cup sweetened
      condensed milk**
   **½ cup butter or margarine,
      softened**
   **½ cup almond brickle
      chips (reserve 2
      teaspoons for garnish)**

GLAZE
   ½ cup confectioners sugar
   1 tablespoon brown sugar
   1 tablespoon milk

1. Preheat oven to 350°F. Grease generously and flour 10-inch Bundt® pan.

2. **For cake,** combine cake mix, pudding mix, eggs, sweetened condensed milk and butter in large bowl. Beat at medium speed with electric mixer for 2 minutes. Fold in brickle chips. Pour into pan. Bake at 350°F for 50 to 60 minutes or until toothpick inserted in center comes out clean. Cool in pan 25 minutes. Invert onto serving plate. Cool completely.

3. **For glaze,** combine confectioners sugar and brown sugar in small bowl. Stir in milk until blended. Drizzle over cake. Sprinkle with reserved almond brickle chips.

Tip: For best results, have all cake ingredients at room temperature before you prepare the batter.

FUDGE MARBLE POUND CAKES

2 Cakes (24 Slices)

1 package Duncan Hines®
Moist Deluxe Fudge
Marble Cake Mix
1 package (4-serving size)
vanilla instant pudding
and pie filling mix
4 eggs
1 cup water
⅓ cup Crisco® Oil or
Crisco® Puritan® Oil

1. Preheat oven to 350°F. Grease and flour two 9×5×3-inch loaf pans.

2. Set aside cocoa packet from Mix. Combine cake mix, pudding mix, eggs, water and oil in large bowl. Beat at medium speed with electric mixer for 2 minutes. Measure 1 cup batter. Place in small bowl; stir in contents of reserved cocoa packet.

3. Spoon half the yellow batter in each loaf pan. Spoon half the chocolate batter on top of yellow batter in each pan. Run knife through batters to marble. Bake at 350°F for 45 to 50 minutes or until toothpick inserted in center comes out clean. Cool in pans 5 minutes. Carefully loosen cakes from pans. Invert onto cooling racks. Cool completely. Cut cakes in slices.

> **Tip:** To make fudge marble ice cream sandwiches, cut ½ gallon brick of fudge marble ice cream into ½-inch slices. Put ice cream slices between slices of pound cake.

Fudge Marble Pound Cake

CITRUS CROWN CAKE

12 to 16 Servings

1 jar (12 ounces) orange
marmalade
⅔ cup flaked coconut
¼ cup butter or margarine,
melted
1 package Duncan Hines®
Moist Deluxe Lemon
Supreme Cake Mix

1. Preheat oven to 350°F. Grease generously and flour 10-inch Bundt® pan.

2. Combine marmalade, coconut and melted butter in small bowl. Pour into pan.

3. Prepare cake following package directions for original recipe. Pour batter over marmalade mixture. Bake at 350°F for 50 to 55 minutes or until toothpick inserted in center comes out clean. Cool in pan 10 minutes. Invert cake onto serving plate. Cool completely.

Tip: For best results, cut cake with a serrated knife; clean after each slice.

PEACHY CINNAMON COFFEECAKE

9 Servings

1 can (8¼ ounces) juice
pack sliced yellow
cling peaches,
undrained
1 package Duncan Hines®
Bakery Style
Cinnamon Swirl
Muffin Mix
1 egg

1. Preheat oven to 400°F. Grease 8-inch square or 9-inch round pan.

2. Drain peaches, reserving juice. Add water to reserved juice to equal ¾ cup liquid. Chop peaches.

3. Combine muffin mix, egg and ¾ cup peach liquid in medium bowl; fold in peaches. Pour into pan. Knead swirl packet from Mix 10 seconds before opening. Squeeze contents on top of batter and swirl with knife. Sprinkle contents of topping from Mix over batter. Bake at 400°F for 28 to 33 minutes for 8-inch pan (20 to 25 minutes for 9-inch pan) or until golden. Serve warm.

Tip: To test the freshness of your eggs, place them in a bowl of cold water. A fresh egg will sink; a stale egg will float.

Citrus Crown Cake

LEMON CHEESE COFFEECAKE

16 to 20 Servings

CAKE
  1 package Duncan Hines®
    Moist Deluxe Lemon
    Supreme Cake Mix,
    divided
  2 eggs
  1 cup all-purpose flour
  1 package active dry yeast
  ⅔ cup warm water

FILLING
  2 packages (8 ounces
    each) cream cheese,
    softened
  2 eggs
  ¼ cup granulated sugar
  1 tablespoon all-purpose
    flour
  1 tablespoon milk

TOPPING
  ¼ cup *plus* 2 tablespoons
    butter or margarine,
    softened

GLAZE
  1 cup confectioners sugar
  1 tablespoon corn syrup
  1 tablespoon water

1. Preheat oven to 350°F. Grease 13×9×2-inch pan.

2. **For cake,** combine 1½ cups cake mix, 2 eggs, 1 cup flour, yeast and ⅔ cup warm water in large bowl. Beat at medium speed with electric mixer for 2 minutes. Spread in pan.

3. **For filling,** combine cream cheese, 2 eggs, granulated sugar, 1 tablespoon flour and milk in small bowl. Beat at low speed with electric mixer until blended. Spoon filling to cover batter.

4. **For topping,** mix remaining cake mix and butter until crumbly. Sprinkle over filling. Bake at 350°F for 40 to 45 minutes or until golden brown.

5. **For glaze,** combine confectioners sugar, corn syrup and 1 tablespoon water in small bowl until smooth. Drizzle over hot coffeecake. Serve warm.

Tip: Also delicious using Duncan Hines® Moist Deluxe Yellow Cake Mix. Substitute 1 tablespoon lemon juice for the 1 tablespoon milk in filling.

DEEP DISH APPLE COBBLER

12 to 16 Servings

CRUST and TOPPING
  1 package Duncan Hines®
    Moist Deluxe Yellow
    Cake Mix
  1 cup quick-cooking oats
    (not instant or
    old-fashioned)
  1 cup chopped walnuts
  ¾ cup butter or margarine,
    melted

1. Preheat oven to 350°F. Grease and flour 13×9×2-inch pan.

2. **For crust and topping,** combine cake mix, oats, walnuts and melted butter in large bowl. Sprinkle half the mixture into pan.

(continued)

FILLING

7½ cups peeled and sliced
     apples (about 6 large)
½ cup raisins
½ cup water
3 tablespoons sugar
2 teaspoons ground
     cinnamon
½ teaspoon ground nutmeg

3. **For filling,** combine apples, raisins, water, sugar, cinnamon and nutmeg in large saucepan. Stir occasionally on low heat for 10 minutes. Spread filling over crust in pan. Sprinkle remaining topping mixture over filling. Bake at 350°F for 35 minutes or until lightly browned. Serve warm or at room temperature.

Tip: For a quick and easy preparation, filling can be heated in the microwave oven. Microwave at HIGH (100% power) for 6 minutes, stirring once.

MILK CHOCOLATE CHEESECAKE

8 Servings

1 package Duncan Hines®
     Moist Deluxe Fudge
     Marble Cake Mix,
     divided
2 packages (8 ounces
     each) cream cheese,
     softened
8 ounces milk chocolate,
     melted
3 eggs
⅔ cup whipping cream
¼ cup *plus* 1 tablespoon
     butter or margarine,
     melted
     Whipped cream, for
     garnish
     Fresh strawberries, for
     garnish

1. Preheat oven to 350°F. Grease and flour 13×9×2-inch pan.

2. For filling, combine contents of cocoa packet from Mix, ¼ cup cake mix, cream cheese and melted chocolate in large bowl. Beat at high speed with electric mixer for 2 minutes. Add eggs and cream. Beat at high speed for 1 minute. Set aside.

3. For crust, stir remaining cake mix and melted butter in medium bowl. Mixture will be crumbly. Sprinkle mixture into pan. Pour filling over crust mixture. Bake at 350°F for 30 to 35 minutes. Cool in pan. Refrigerate until chilled. Garnish individual servings with dollops of whipped cream and strawberries.

Tip: Cheesecake may be soft in the center, but will become firm as it chills.

Especially Elegant

LINZER HEARTS

22 (3-inch) Sandwich Cookies

1 package Duncan Hines®
   Golden Sugar
   Cookie Mix
½ cup all-purpose flour
½ cup finely ground
   almonds
1 egg
1 tablespoon water
3 tablespoons
   confectioners sugar
½ cup *plus* 1 tablespoon
   seedless red raspberry
   jam, warmed

1. Preheat oven to 375°F.

2. Combine cookie mix, contents of buttery flavor packet from Mix, flour, almonds, egg and water in large bowl. Stir with spoon until blended. Roll dough ⅛ inch thick on lightly floured board. Cut out 3-inch hearts with floured cookie cutter. Cut out centers of half the hearts with smaller heart cookie cutter. Reroll dough as needed. Place 2 inches apart on ungreased baking sheets. Bake whole hearts at 375°F for 8 to 9 minutes and cut-out hearts for 6 to 7 minutes or until edges are lightly browned. Cool 1 minute on baking sheets. Remove to cooling racks. Cool completely.

3. To assemble, dust cut-out hearts with sifted confectioners sugar. Spread warm jam over whole hearts almost to edges; top with cut-out hearts. Press together to make sandwiches. Fill center with ¼ teaspoon jam. Store between layers of waxed paper in airtight container.

Tip: If you like a softer cookie, make these a day ahead.

Linzer Hearts

ANGEL STRAWBERRY
BAVARIAN

12 to 16 Servings

1 package Duncan Hines®
   Angel Food Cake Mix
1 package (10 ounces)
   sweetened, frozen
   sliced strawberries,
   thawed
1 package (4-serving size)
   strawberry flavored
   gelatin
1 cup boiling water
2½ cups whipping cream,
   chilled and divided
2½ tablespoons
   confectioners sugar
¾ teaspoon vanilla extract
4 fresh strawberries,
   sliced and fanned, for
   garnish
Mint leaves, for garnish

1. Preheat oven to 375°F.

2. Prepare, bake and cool cake following package directions. Cut cooled cake into 1-inch cubes.

3. Drain thawed strawberries, reserving juice.

4. Combine gelatin and boiling water in small bowl. Stir until gelatin is dissolved. Add enough water to strawberry juice to measure 1 cup; stir into gelatin. Refrigerate until gelatin is slightly thickened. Beat gelatin until foamy.

5. Beat 1 cup whipping cream until stiff peaks form in large bowl. Fold into gelatin along with strawberries.

6. Alternate layers of cake cubes and strawberry mixture in 10-inch tube pan. Press lightly. Cover. Refrigerate overnight.

7. Unmold cake onto serving plate. Beat remaining 1½ cups whipping cream, confectioners sugar and vanilla extract until stiff peaks form. Frost sides and top of cake. Refrigerate until ready to serve. Garnish with fresh strawberries and mint leaves.

Tip: For easiest cutting, use a knife with a thin sharp blade.

Angel Strawberry Bavarian

CHOCOLATE MARBLE CHEESECAKE

12 to 16 Servings

CRUST
1 package Duncan Hines®
    Moist Deluxe Devil's
    Food Cake Mix
½ cup Crisco® Oil or
    Crisco® Puritan® Oil

FILLING
3 packages (8 ounces
    each) cream cheese,
    softened
¾ cup sugar
½ teaspoon almond extract
3 eggs
1 square (1 ounce)
    unsweetened chocolate,
    melted

1. Preheat oven to 350°F. Grease 9-inch springform pan.

2. **For crust,** combine cake mix and oil in large bowl. Stir until well blended. Press mixture into bottom of pan. Bake at 350°F for 22 minutes. Remove from oven. *Increase oven temperature to 450°F.*

3. **For filling,** combine cream cheese, sugar and almond extract in large bowl. Beat at medium speed with electric mixer until blended. Add eggs, one at a time, beating well after each addition. Remove 1 cup batter to small bowl; add melted chocolate. Spoon plain batter into warm crust. Drop spoonfuls of chocolate batter over plain batter. Run knife through batters to marble. Bake at 450°F for 7 minutes. *Reduce oven temperature to 250°F.* Bake for 30 minutes longer or until cheesecake is set. Loosen cake from sides of pan with knife or spatula. Cool completely on rack. Remove sides of pan. Refrigerate until ready to serve.

Tip: To prevent chocolate from turning grainy, melt chocolate in saucepan on very low heat, or melt in 1-cup glass measure in microwave oven at HIGH for 1 to 1½ minutes (stir to make sure chocolate is melted).

Chocolate Marble Cheesecake

LIGHT AND LUSCIOUS
LEMON CAKE

12 to 16 Servings

**1 package Duncan Hines®
   Moist Deluxe Lemon
   Supreme Cake Mix**

FROSTING
**1 can (6 ounces) frozen
   lemonade concentrate,
   thawed**
**1 can (14 ounces)
   sweetened condensed
   milk**
**1 container (8 ounces)
   frozen whipped
   topping, thawed**
**3 drops yellow food
   coloring (optional)**
**Lemon slices, for
   garnish**
Mint leaves, for garnish

1. Preheat oven to 350°F. Grease and flour 13×9×2-inch pan.

2. Prepare and bake cake following package directions for original recipe. Cool in pan 15 minutes. Invert onto cooling rack. Cool completely. Split cake in half horizontally (see Tip).

3. **For frosting,** combine lemonade concentrate and sweetened condensed milk in medium bowl. Fold in whipped topping. Add food coloring, if desired. Blend well. Place bottom cake layer on serving plate. Spread one-third frosting on top. Place top cake layer on frosting. Frost sides and top with remaining frosting. Garnish with lemon slices and mint leaves. Refrigerate until ready to serve.

Tip: To cut cake evenly, measure cake with ruler. Divide into 2 equal layers. Mark with toothpicks. Cut through layer with large serrated knife using toothpicks as guide.

Light and Luscious Lemon Cake

CHOCOLATE ANGEL
FOOD ROLLS

16 to 20 Servings

CAKE
  **1 package Duncan Hines®
    Angel Food Cake Mix**
  **3 tablespoons
    unsweetened cocoa**
  Confectioners sugar

FILLING
  **½ square grated semi-
    sweet chocolate**
  **1 container (8 ounces)
    frozen whipped
    topping, thawed**

DRIZZLE
  **2 squares (2 ounces) semi-
    sweet chocolate,
    chopped**
  **2 teaspoons Crisco®
    Shortening**

1. Preheat oven to 350°F. Line two 15½×10½×1-inch jelly-roll pans with aluminum foil.

2. **For cake,** combine Cake Flour Mixture (red "B" packet) and cocoa in small bowl. Prepare cake following package directions. Divide batter into pans. Spread evenly. Cut through batter with knife or spatula to remove large air bubbles. Bake at 350°F for 15 minutes or until set. Invert cakes at once onto lint-free kitchen towels dusted with confectioners sugar. Remove foil carefully. Starting at short end, roll up each cake with towel jelly-roll fashion. Cool completely.

3. **For filling,** fold grated chocolate into whipped topping. Unroll cakes. Spread half of filling to edges on each cake. Reroll and place seam-side down on serving plate.

4. **For drizzle,** combine chopped chocolate and shortening in small resealable plastic bag. Place bag in bowl of hot water for several minutes. Dry with paper towel. Knead until blended and chocolate is smooth. Snip pinpoint hole in corner of bag. Drizzle over rolls. Refrigerate until ready to serve.

Tip: For a quick finish, omit drizzle; simply dust angel food rolls with confectioners sugar.

Chocolate Angel Food Roll

PRALINE CHEESECAKE

12 to 16 Servings

CRUST
  1 package Duncan Hines®
    Moist Deluxe Spice
    Cake Mix
  ½ cup Crisco® Oil or
    Crisco® Puritan® Oil
  ⅓ cup chopped pecans
FILLING
  3 packages (8 ounces
    each) cream cheese,
    softened
  1¼ cups firmly packed
    brown sugar
  2 tablespoons all-purpose
    flour
  3 eggs, lightly beaten
  1½ teaspoons vanilla
    extract
  ½ cup finely chopped
    pecans
  2 tablespoons maple
    syrup, for glaze
    Pecan halves, for
    garnish

1. Preheat oven to 350°F. Grease 9-inch springform pan.

2. **For crust,** combine cake mix, oil and ⅓ cup pecans in large bowl. Mix well. Press into bottom of pan. Bake at 350°F for 20 to 23 minutes. Remove from oven. *Increase oven temperature to 450°F.*

3. **For filling,** place cream cheese in large bowl. Beat at low speed with electric mixer adding brown sugar and flour gradually. Add eggs and vanilla extract, mixing only until incorporated. Fold in ½ cup pecans. Pour filling onto crust. Bake at 450°F for 5 to 7 minutes. *Reduce oven temperature to 250°F.* Bake for 35 to 40 minutes longer or until set. Loosen cake from sides of pan with knife or spatula. Cool completely on cooling rack. Refrigerate 2 hours or until ready to serve. Remove sides of pan.

4. To serve, brush top with maple syrup. Garnish with pecan halves.

Tip: Oven temperature is reduced to prevent cheesecake from cracking.

MOCHA WALNUT BROWNIE TORTE

12 Servings

BROWNIES
  1 package Duncan Hines®
    Brownies Plus
    Walnuts Mix
  2 eggs
  ⅓ cup water
  ⅓ cup Crisco® Oil or
    Crisco® Puritan® Oil

1. Preheat oven to 350°F. Grease and flour two 9-inch round cake pans.

2. **For brownies,** combine brownie mix, eggs, water and oil in large bowl. Stir with spoon until well blended, about 50 strokes. Spread in pans. Bake at 350°F for 20 minutes. Cool in pans 5 minutes. Invert onto cooling racks. Cool completely.

(continued)

FILLING and FROSTING
  **2 cups whipping cream,
    chilled**
  **½ cup firmly packed brown
    sugar**
  1 tablespoon *plus*
    **1 teaspoon Folgers®
    Coffee Crystals**
  Walnuts, for garnish
  **Chocolate shavings, for
    garnish**

3. **For filling and frosting,** beat whipping cream in medium bowl until soft peaks form. Add brown sugar and coffee gradually. Beat until stiff peaks form. Fill and frost sides and top of brownie layers. Garnish with walnuts and chocolate shavings (see Tip).

Tip: To prepare chocolate shavings, place a piece of waxed paper under a box style grater. Pass a square of chocolate across the shredding holes of the grater.

ORANGE PECAN LOAVES

2 Loaves (24 Slices)

LOAVES
  **1 package Duncan Hines®
    Moist Deluxe White
    Cake Mix**
  3 eggs
  **1¼ cups Citrus Hill®
    Orange Juice**
  **⅓ cup Crisco® Oil or
    Crisco® Puritan® Oil**
  **½ cup finely chopped
    pecans**
GLAZE
  ½ cup confectioners sugar
  **1 tablespoon Citrus Hill®
    Orange Juice**
  **Pecan halves, for
    garnish**
  **Orange slices, for
    garnish**

1. Preheat oven to 350°F. Grease and flour two 8½×4½×2½-inch loaf pans.

2. **For loaves,** combine cake mix, eggs, 1¼ cups orange juice and oil in large bowl. Beat at medium speed with electric mixer for 2 minutes. Stir in chopped pecans. Pour into pans. Bake at 350°F for 40 to 45 minutes or until toothpick inserted in center comes out clean. Cool in pans 15 minutes. Loosen loaves from pans. Invert onto cooling racks. Turn right-side up. Cool completely.

3. **For glaze,** combine confectioners sugar and 1 tablespoon orange juice in small bowl. Stir until smooth. Drizzle over cooled loaves. Garnish with pecan halves and orange slices.

Tip: Freeze one loaf to be served at a later time. Wrap loaf tightly in plastic. Frozen loaf will keep up to 6 weeks.

LEMON COOKIES

3 Dozen Cookies

1 package Duncan Hines®
Moist Deluxe Lemon
Supreme Cake Mix
2 eggs
⅓ cup Crisco® Oil or
Crisco® Puritan® Oil
1 tablespoon lemon juice
¾ cup chopped nuts or
flaked coconut
Confectioners sugar

1. Preheat oven to 375°F. Grease baking sheets.

2. Combine cake mix, eggs, oil and lemon juice in large bowl. Beat at low speed with electric mixer until well blended. Add nuts. Shape into 36 (1-inch) balls. Place 2 inches apart on baking sheets. Bake at 375°F for 6 to 7 minutes or until set. Cool 1 minute on baking sheets. Remove to cooling racks. Cool completely. Dust with confectioners sugar. Store in airtight container.

Tip: You can frost cookies with 1 cup confectioners sugar mixed with 1 tablespoon lemon juice in place of dusting cookies with confectioners sugar.

MOCHA FUDGE CAKE

12 to 16 Servings

1 package Duncan Hines®
Moist Deluxe Butter
Recipe Fudge
Cake Mix
1 cup hot fudge ice cream
topping
1 tablespoon Folgers®
Coffee Crystals
4 cups frozen whipped
topping, thawed and
divided

1. Preheat oven to 375°F. Grease and flour two 9-inch round cake pans.

2. Prepare, bake and cool cake following package directions for original recipe.

3. For filling, combine hot fudge topping and coffee in medium saucepan. Heat until coffee is dissolved. Cool. Fold 2 cups whipped topping into fudge topping mixture. Refrigerate 30 minutes.

4. Place one cake layer on serving plate. Spread with 1 cup filling. Top with second cake layer. Add remaining 2 cups whipped topping to remaining filling. Frost sides and top of cake with topping mixture.

Tip: Garnish with chocolate curls, coated coffee beans or grated chocolate.

Lemon Cookies

CHOCOLATE TOFFEE FANTASY

12 Servings

1 package Duncan Hines®
Moist Deluxe Devil's
Food Cake Mix
12 bars (1.4 ounces each)
chocolate covered
toffee bars, divided
3 cups whipping cream,
chilled

1. Preheat oven to 350°F. Grease and flour 10-inch tube pan.

2. Prepare, bake and cool cake following package directions for original recipe. Split cake horizontally into three layers. Chop 11 candy bars into pea-size pieces (see Tip). Whip cream until stiff peaks form. Fold candy pieces into whipped cream.

3. To assemble, place one split cake layer on serving plate. Spread 1½ cups whipped cream mixture on top. Repeat with remaining layers and whipped cream mixture. Frost sides and top with remaining whipped cream mixture. Chop remaining candy bar coarsely. Sprinkle over top. Refrigerate until ready to serve.

Tip: To quickly chop toffee candy bars, place a few bars in food processor fitted with steel blade. Pulse several times until pea-size pieces form. Repeat with remaining candy bars.

COCONUT FUDGE TORTE

12 Servings

1 package Duncan Hines®
Moist Deluxe Butter
Recipe Fudge
Cake Mix
1 container (16 ounces)
dairy sour cream
2 cups sugar
2¼ cups flaked coconut,
divided

1. Preheat oven to 375°F. Grease and flour two 9-inch round cake pans.

2. Prepare, bake and cool cake following package directions for original recipe. Split each cake layer in half horizontally.

3. Combine sour cream, sugar and 2 cups coconut in large bowl. Place one split cake layer on serving plate. Spread 1 cup filling on top. Repeat with remaining cake layers and filling. Sprinkle with remaining ¼ cup coconut. Refrigerate until ready to serve.

Tip: Garnish with chocolate curls, if desired.

Chocolate Toffee Fantasy

12 Servings

CAKE
**1 package Duncan Hines®
Moist Deluxe Yellow
Cake Mix**
**1 jar (18 ounces) apricot
preserves, divided**

FROSTING
**1 package (4-serving size)
vanilla instant pudding
and pie filling mix**
¾ cup milk
**1½ cups whipping cream,
chilled**
**¼ cup flaked coconut, for
garnish**
**Apricot halves, for
garnish**
Mint leaves, for garnish

1. Preheat oven to 350°F. Grease and flour two 9-inch round cake pans.

2. **For cake,** prepare, bake and cool following package directions for original recipe. Split each cake layer in half horizontally. Reserve 1 tablespoon preserves. Place one split cake layer on serving plate. Spread one-third of remaining preserves on top. Repeat with remaining layers and preserves, leaving top plain.

3. **For frosting,** prepare pudding mix following package directions using ¾ cup milk. Beat whipping cream until stiff in large bowl. Fold whipped cream into pudding. Spread on sides and top of cake. Garnish with coconut, apricot halves and mint leaves. Warm reserved preserves to glaze apricot halves. Refrigerate until ready to serve.

Tip: Three cups thawed frozen whipped topping may be substituted for whipping cream. A wire whisk is helpful when folding whipped cream into pudding.

Apricot Cream Cake

BANANA CHOCOLATE CHIP PARFAITS

6 Parfaits

1 package Duncan Hines®
    Chocolate Chip
    Cookie Mix

PUDDING

3 tablespoons cornstarch
¼ teaspoon salt
1⅔ cups water
1 can (14 ounces)
    sweetened condensed
    milk
3 egg yolks, beaten
2 tablespoons butter or
    margarine
1½ teaspoons vanilla
    extract
3 ripe bananas, sliced
    Whipped topping, for
    garnish
    Mint leaves, for garnish

1. Preheat oven to 375°F. Grease 13×9×2-inch pan.

2. Prepare cookie mix following package directions for original recipe. Spread in pan. Bake at 375°F for 15 to 18 minutes or until edges are light golden brown. Cool.

3. **For pudding,** combine cornstarch, salt and water in medium saucepan. Add sweetened condensed milk and egg yolks. Cook over medium heat, stirring constantly, until thickened. Remove from heat. Stir in butter and vanilla extract. Cool.

4. To assemble, cut outer edges from cookie bars. Crumble to make about 1¾ cups crumbs. Layer pudding, banana slices and crumbs in parfait dishes. Repeat layers 1 or 2 more times ending with pudding. Garnish with whipped topping and mint leaves. Refrigerate until ready to serve.

Tip: Cut remaining cookie bars into 1×2-inch pieces. Serve with parfaits.

Banana Chocolate Chip Parfaits

8 Servings

CAKE

**1 package Duncan Hines®
Moist Deluxe Devil's
Food Cake Mix**

3 eggs

1⅓ cups water

**⅓ cup Crisco® Oil or
Crisco® Puritan® Oil**

¼ cup whipping cream

**2 tablespoons
unsweetened cocoa**

FROSTING

**8 ounces sweet chocolate,
melted and cooled**

**¼ cup butter or margarine,
chilled**

**¼ cup whipping cream,
chilled**

MOUSSE

**2 cups whipping cream,
chilled**

**½ cup confectioners sugar,
sifted**

**⅓ cup unsweetened cocoa,
sifted**

TOPPING

**½ cup whipping cream,
chilled**

**¼ cup confectioners sugar
Milk chocolate stars or
kisses, for garnish**

1. Preheat oven to 350°F. Grease and flour two 9-inch round cake pans (see Tip).

2. **For cake,** combine cake mix, eggs, water, oil, ¼ cup whipping cream and 2 tablespoons cocoa in large bowl. Beat at medium speed with electric mixer for 2 minutes. Pour into pans. Bake and cool cake following package directions. Freeze one cake layer for later use.

3. **For frosting,** combine melted chocolate, butter and ¼ cup whipping cream in small bowl. Beat at high speed with electric mixer for 1 minute. Frost sides and top of cake layer. Refrigerate 30 minutes.

4. **For mousse,** combine 2 cups whipping cream, ½ cup confectioners sugar and ⅓ cup cocoa in medium bowl. Beat at high speed with electric mixer for 2 minutes or until stiff. Spread evenly over sides and top of frosted cake. Refrigerate.

5. **For topping,** combine ½ cup whipping cream and ¼ cup confectioners sugar in medium bowl. Beat at high speed with electric mixer for 1 to 2 minutes or until stiff. Dollop around outer top edge to form a ring. Garnish with chocolate stars. Refrigerate until ready to serve.

Tip: Instead of baking the second cake layer, prepare 12 cupcakes for the kids.

Chocolate Elegance Cake

CHOCOLATE CHERRY CAKE

12 to 16 Servings

**1 package Duncan Hines®
Moist Deluxe Devil's
Food Cake Mix**
**½ cup chopped maraschino
cherries, well drained**
**2 cups frozen whipped
topping, thawed**
**1 container (16 ounces)
Duncan Hines®
Chocolate Layer Cake
Frosting**

1. Preheat oven to 350°F. Grease and flour two 9-inch round cake pans.

2. Prepare, bake and cool cake following package directions for original recipe. Fold maraschino cherries into whipped topping.

3. To assemble, place one cake layer on serving plate. Spread with whipped topping mixture. Top with second layer. Frost sides and top with Chocolate frosting. Refrigerate until ready to serve.

Tip: Fresh or canned dark sweet cherries, well drained, can be used in place of maraschino cherries.

LEMON CHEESECAKE WITH RASPBERRY SAUCE

12 to 16 Servings

CRUST
**1 package Duncan Hines®
Moist Deluxe Lemon
Supreme Cake Mix**
**½ cup Crisco® Oil or
Crisco® Puritan® Oil**
**⅓ cup finely chopped
pecans**

FILLING
**3 packages (8 ounces
each) cream cheese,
softened**
¾ cup sugar
2 tablespoons lemon juice
**1 teaspoon grated lemon
peel**
3 eggs, lightly beaten

1. Preheat oven to 350°F. Grease 10-inch springform pan.

2. **For crust,** combine cake mix and oil in large bowl. Mix well. Stir in pecans. Press mixture into bottom of pan. Bake at 350°F for about 20 minutes or until light golden brown. Remove from oven. *Increase oven temperature to 450°F.*

3. **For filling,** place cream cheese in large bowl. Beat at low speed with electric mixer, adding ¾ cup sugar gradually. Add lemon juice and lemon peel. Add eggs, mixing only until incorporated. Pour filling onto crust. Bake at 450°F for 5 to 7 minutes. *Reduce oven temperature to 250°F.* Bake for 30 minutes longer or until set. Loosen cake from sides of pan with knife or spatula. Cool completely on cooling rack. Refrigerate 2 hours or until ready to serve. Remove sides of pan.

(continued)

RASPBERRY SAUCE
1 package (12 ounces)
frozen dry pack red
raspberries, thawed
⅓ cup sugar
Fresh raspberries, for
garnish
Lemon slices, for
garnish
Mint leaves, for garnish

4. **For raspberry sauce,** combine thawed raspberries and ⅓ cup sugar in small saucepan. Bring to a boil. Simmer until berries are soft. Strain through sieve into small bowl to remove seeds. Cool completely.

5. To serve, garnish cheesecake with raspberries, lemon slices and mint leaves. Cut into slices and serve with raspberry sauce.

Tip: Overbeating cheesecake batter can incorporate too much air, which may cause the cheesecake to crack during baking.

BLACK FOREST TORTE

12 to 16 Servings

1 package Duncan Hines®
Moist Deluxe Dark
Dutch Fudge
Cake Mix
2½ cups whipping cream,
chilled
2½ tablespoons
confectioners sugar
1 can (21 ounces) cherry
pie filling

1. Preheat oven to 350°F. Grease and flour two 9-inch round cake pans.

2. Prepare, bake and cool cake following package directions for original recipe.

3. Beat whipping cream in large bowl until soft peaks form. Add confectioners sugar gradually. Beat until stiff peaks form.

4. To assemble, place one cake layer on serving plate. Spread two-thirds cherry pie filling on cake to within ½ inch of edge. Spread 1½ cups whipped cream mixture over cherry pie filling. Top with second cake layer. Frost sides and top with remaining whipped cream mixture. Spread remaining cherry pie filling on top to within 1 inch of edge. Refrigerate until ready to serve.

Tip: Garnish with grated semi-sweet chocolate.

CHERRY SURPRISES

3 to 3½ Dozen Cookies

1 package Duncan Hines®
  Golden Sugar
  Cookie Mix
36 to 42 candied cherries
½ cup semi-sweet
  chocolate chips
1 teaspoon Crisco®
  Shortening

1. Preheat oven to 375°F. Grease baking sheets.

2. Prepare cookie mix following package directions for original recipe. Shape thin layer of dough around each candied cherry. Place 2 inches apart on baking sheets. Bake at 375°F for 8 minutes or until set but not browned. Cool 1 minute on baking sheets. Remove to cooling racks. Cool completely.

3. Combine chocolate chips and shortening in small resealable plastic bag. Place bag in bowl of hot water for several minutes. Dry with paper towel. Knead until blended and chocolate is smooth. Snip pinpoint hole in corner of bag. Drizzle chocolate over cookies. Allow drizzle to set before storing between layers of waxed paper in airtight container.

> **Tip:** Well-drained maraschino cherries may be substituted for candied cherries.

Cherry Surprises

16 Servings

CRUST
  1 package Duncan Hines®
    Moist Deluxe Swiss
    Chocolate Cake Mix
  ¾ cup butter or margarine,
    softened

1st LAYER
  1 package (8 ounces)
    cream cheese, softened
  1 cup confectioners sugar
  1 cup frozen whipped
    topping, thawed

2nd LAYER
  2 packages (4-serving size
    each) chocolate instant
    pudding and pie
    filling mix
  3 cups milk

3rd LAYER
  2 cups frozen whipped
    topping, thawed
    Chocolate leaves, for
    garnish (optional)
    Mint leaves, for garnish
    (optional)

1. Preheat oven to 350°F. Grease two 9-inch pie pans.

2. **For crust,** place cake mix in large bowl. Cut in butter with pastry blender or 2 knives. Put half the crumbs in each pan. Press up sides and on bottom of each pan. Bake at 350°F for 15 minutes. Cool.

3. **For 1st layer,** combine cream cheese and confectioners sugar in small bowl. Beat at medium speed with electric mixer until smooth. Stir in 1 cup whipped topping. Spread half the mixture evenly over each crust. Refrigerate.

4. **For 2nd layer,** prepare pudding mixes following package directions using 3 cups milk. Spoon half the pudding over cream cheese mixture in each pan.

5. **For 3rd layer,** spread 1 cup whipped topping on each pie. Refrigerate until ready to serve. Garnish with chocolate and mint leaves, if desired.

Note: One container (8 ounces) frozen whipped topping will be enough for recipe.

Tip: For **Heavenly Lemon Cream Pies** use Duncan Hines® Moist Deluxe Lemon Supreme Cake Mix in place of Swiss Chocolate Cake Mix and lemon instant pudding and pie filling mix in place of chocolate pudding and pie filling mix.

Heavenly Chocolate Cream Pie

CHOCOLATE CHIP CHEESECAKE

12 to 16 Servings

CRUST
  **1 package Duncan Hines®
    Moist Deluxe Devil's
    Food Cake Mix**
  **½ cup Crisco® Oil or
    Crisco® Puritan® Oil**

FILLING
  **3 packages (8 ounces
    each) cream cheese,
    softened**
  1½ cups sugar
  1 cup dairy sour cream
  **1½ teaspoons vanilla
    extract**
  4 eggs, lightly beaten
  **¾ cup semi-sweet mini
    chocolate chips,
    divided**
  **1 teaspoon all-purpose
    flour**

1. Preheat oven to 350°F. Grease 10-inch springform pan.

2. **For crust,** combine cake mix and oil in large bowl. Mix well. Press into bottom of pan. Bake at 350°F for 22 to 25 minutes. Remove from oven. *Increase oven temperature to 450°F.*

3. **For filling,** place cream cheese in large bowl. Beat at low speed with electric mixer adding sugar gradually. Add sour cream and vanilla extract, mixing until blended. Add eggs, mixing only until incorporated. Toss ½ cup chocolate chips with flour. Fold into cream cheese mixture. Pour filling onto crust. Sprinkle with remaining ¼ cup chocolate chips. Bake at 450°F for 5 to 7 minutes. *Reduce oven temperature to 250°F.* Bake for 60 to 65 minutes longer or until set. Loosen cake from sides of pan with knife or spatula. Cool completely on cooling rack. Refrigerate until ready to serve. Remove sides of pan.

Tip: Place pan of water on bottom shelf of oven during baking to prevent cheesecake from cracking.

Chocolate Chip Cheesecake

DELICATE WHITE CHOCOLATE CAKE

12 to 16 Servings

CAKE
 1 package Duncan Hines®
    Moist Deluxe White
    Cake Mix
 1 package (4-serving size)
    vanilla instant pudding
    and pie filling mix
 4 egg whites
 1 cup water
 ½ cup Crisco® Oil or
    Crisco® Puritan® Oil
 5 ounces finely chopped
    white chocolate

FILLING
 1 cup cherry preserves
 8 drops red food coloring
    (optional)

FROSTING
 2 cups whipping cream,
    chilled
 2 tablespoons
    confectioners sugar
    Maraschino cherries,
    for garnish
 1 ounce white chocolate
    shavings, for garnish
    (see Tip)

1. Preheat oven to 350°F. Cut waxed paper circles to fit bottoms of three 9-inch round cake pans. Grease bottoms and sides of pans. Line with waxed paper circles.

2. **For cake,** combine cake mix, pudding mix, egg whites, water and oil in large bowl. Beat at medium speed with electric mixer for 2 minutes. Fold in chopped white chocolate. Pour into pans. Bake at 350°F for 18 to 22 minutes. Cool in pans 15 minutes. Invert onto cooling racks. Peel off waxed paper. Cool completely.

3. **For filling,** combine cherry preserves and food coloring, if desired. Stir to blend color.

4. **For frosting,** beat whipping cream in large bowl until soft peaks form. Add confectioners sugar gradually. Beat until stiff peaks form.

5. To assemble, place one cake layer on serving plate. Spread ½ cup cherry preserves over cake. Place second cake layer on top. Spread with remaining preserves. Place third cake layer on top. Frost sides and top of cake with whipped cream. Decorate with maraschino cherries and white chocolate shavings. Refrigerate until ready to serve.

Tip: To make white chocolate shavings, use sharp vegetable peeler to slice across square of chocolate.

Delicate White Chocolate Cake

12 Servings

1 package Duncan Hines® Moist Deluxe Dark Dutch Fudge Cake Mix

1 package (6 ounces) semi-sweet chocolate chips, melted, for garnish

1 container (8 ounces) frozen whipped topping, thawed and divided

1 container (16 ounces) Duncan Hines® Milk Chocolate Layer Cake Frosting

3 tablespoons finely chopped dry roasted pistachios

1. Preheat oven to 350°F. Grease and flour two 9-inch round cake pans.

2. Prepare, bake and cool cake following package directions for original recipe.

3. For chocolate hearts garnish, spread melted chocolate to ⅛-inch thickness on waxed-paper-lined baking sheet. Cut shapes with heart cookie cutter when chocolate begins to set. Refrigerate until firm. Push out heart shapes. Set aside.

4. To assemble, split each cake layer in half horizontally. Place one split cake layer on serving plate. Spread one-third whipped topping on top. Repeat with remaining layers and whipped topping, leaving top plain. Frost sides and top with Milk Chocolate frosting. Sprinkle pistachios on top. Position chocolate hearts by pushing points down into cake. Refrigerate until ready to serve.

Tip: To make **Chocolate Strawberry Dream Torte,** omit semi-sweet chocolate chips and chopped pistachios. Proceed as above through step #2. Fold 1½ cups chopped fresh strawberries into whipped topping in large bowl. Assemble as above, filling cake with strawberry mixture. Garnish cake with fresh strawberry fans and mint leaves.

Chocolate Dream Torte

ORANGE COCONUT FUDGE CAKE

12 to 16 Servings

1 can (6 ounces) Citrus Hill® Frozen Orange Juice concentrate, thawed

CAKE
  1 package Duncan Hines® Moist Deluxe Butter Recipe Fudge Cake Mix
  ¾ cup Citrus Hill® Orange Juice (see step #2)
  3 eggs
  ½ cup butter or margarine, softened
  2 tablespoons orange liqueur (optional)

FROSTING
  1 cup evaporated milk
  ¾ cup sugar
  3 egg yolks
  ¼ cup butter or margarine
  2 tablespoons Citrus Hill® Frozen Orange Juice concentrate, reserved from above
  1 teaspoon vanilla extract
  2 cups chopped pecans
  1 cup flaked coconut

1. Preheat oven to 375°F. Grease and flour two 9-inch round cake pans.

2. Measure 2 tablespoons orange juice concentrate. Set aside for frosting. Reconstitute remaining concentrate using ⅓ cup less water than package directions; reserve ¾ cup for cake.

3. **For cake,** combine cake mix, reserved orange juice, 3 eggs, ½ cup butter and liqueur, if desired, in large bowl. Beat at medium speed with electric mixer for 4 minutes. Pour into pans. Bake and cool cake following package directions.

4. **For frosting,** combine evaporated milk, sugar, egg yolks and ¼ cup butter in medium saucepan. Cook on medium heat, stirring constantly, until mixture comes to a boil and thickens. Remove from heat. Stir in reserved orange juice concentrate and vanilla extract. Add pecans and coconut. Cool. Place one cake layer on serving plate. Spread with thin layer of frosting. Top with second cake layer. Frost sides and top with remaining frosting. Refrigerate until ready to serve.

Tip: Garnish cake with orange slices or twists, if desired.

REFRESHING LEMON LAYERS

12 to 16 Servings

1 package Duncan Hines® Moist Deluxe Lemon Supreme Cake Mix

FILLING
  1 package (4-serving size) lemon instant pudding and pie filling mix
  1½ cups milk

1. Preheat oven to 350°F. Grease and flour two 9-inch round cake pans.

2. Prepare, bake and cool cake following package directions for original recipe.

3. **For filling,** prepare pudding mix following package directions using 1½ cups milk. Refrigerate.

(continued)

FROSTING
   2 cups whipping cream,
      chilled
   ⅓ cup sugar
   1¾ teaspoons grated lemon
      peel
   Lemon slices, for
      garnish
   Mint leaves, for garnish

4. **For frosting,** beat whipping cream in large bowl until soft peaks form. Add sugar gradually. Beat until stiff peaks form. Fold in lemon peel.

5. To assemble, split each cake layer in half horizontally. Place one split cake layer on serving plate. Spread ½ cup lemon filling on top. Repeat with remaining layers and lemon filling, leaving top plain. Frost sides and top with whipped cream frosting. Garnish with fresh lemon slices and mint leaves. Refrigerate until ready to serve.

> **Tip:** Cakes filled and frosted with whipped toppings are easier to cut if refrigerated several hours before serving.

CHOCOLATE ROYALE

12 to 16 Servings

1 package Duncan Hines®
   Moist Deluxe Devil's
   Food Cake Mix
FROSTING
   1 package (3 ounces)
      cream cheese, softened
   ½ cup confectioners sugar
   1 teaspoon vanilla extract
   1 cup whipping cream,
      whipped
   2 large bananas, sliced
      Lemon juice
      Chocolate sprinkles

1. Preheat oven to 350°F. Grease and flour two 8-inch round cake pans.

2. Prepare, bake and cool cake following package directions for original recipe.

3. **For frosting,** combine cream cheese, confectioners sugar and vanilla extract in small bowl. Beat at low speed with electric mixer until blended. Fold whipped cream into cheese mixture.

4. To assemble, place one cake layer on serving plate. Spread with thin layer of frosting. Reserve 12 banana slices for garnish; dip in lemon juice. Cover frosted layer with remaining banana slices. Spread another thin layer of frosting over bananas. Place second cake layer on top. Frost sides and top with remaining frosting. Blot reserved banana slices dry on paper towel. Roll banana slices in chocolate sprinkles. Garnish top of cake with banana slices. Refrigerate until ready to serve.

> **Tip:** To keep plate neat when frosting a layer cake, tuck four strips of waxed paper under edges of the bottom cake layer; carefully remove waxed paper.

Harvest Bounty

RICH PUMPKIN CHEESECAKE

12 to 16 Servings

CRUST
1 package Duncan Hines®
   Moist Deluxe Spice
   Cake Mix
½ cup butter or margarine,
   melted

FILLING
3 packages (8 ounces
   each) cream cheese,
   softened
1 can (14 ounces)
   sweetened condensed
   milk
1 can (16 ounces) solid
   pack pumpkin
4 eggs
1 tablespoon pumpkin pie
   spice

TOPPING
1 package (2½ ounces)
   sliced almonds
2 cups whipping cream,
   chilled
¼ cup sugar

1. Preheat oven to 375°F.

2. **For crust,** combine cake mix and melted butter in large bowl; press in bottom of ungreased 10-inch springform pan.

3. **For filling,** combine cream cheese and sweetened condensed milk in large bowl. Beat at high speed with electric mixer for 2 minutes. Add pumpkin, eggs and pumpkin pie spice. Beat at high speed for 1 minute. Pour over crust in pan. Bake at 375°F for 65 to 70 minutes or until set. Loosen cake from sides of pan with knife or spatula. Cool completely on rack. Refrigerate 2 hours. Remove sides of pan.

4. **For topping,** preheat oven to 300°F. Toast almonds on baking sheet at 300°F for 4 to 5 minutes or until fragrant and light golden brown. Cool completely. Beat cream in medium bowl until soft peaks form. Gradually add sugar; beat until stiff peaks form. Spread over top of chilled cheesecake. Garnish with toasted almonds. Refrigerate until ready to serve.

Tip: To prepare in a 13×9×2-inch pan, bake at 350°F for 35 minutes or until set.

Rich Pumpkin Cheesecake

OATMEAL APPLESAUCE SQUARES

12 Bars

1 package Duncan Hines®
  Moist Deluxe Spice
  Cake Mix
2 eggs
½ cup butter or margarine,
  softened
2 cups applesauce
1 cup quick-cooking oats
  (not instant or
  old-fashioned)
½ cup firmly packed brown
  sugar

1. Preheat oven to 350°F. Grease 13×9×2-inch pan.

2. Combine cake mix, eggs and butter in large bowl. Beat at low speed with electric mixer until blended. Spread in pan. Bake at 350°F for 15 minutes. Pour applesauce over hot baked layer.

3. Combine oats and brown sugar in small bowl. Mix until crumbly. Sprinkle over applesauce. Return to oven. Bake for 10 minutes longer or until lightly browned. Cool. Cut into squares.

Tip: You can use flavored applesauce in place of regular applesauce.

PUMPKIN STREUSEL CAKE

16 to 20 Servings

STREUSEL
  1 cup firmly packed brown
    sugar
  2 teaspoons ground
    cinnamon
  ⅓ cup butter or margarine,
    softened
  1 cup chopped nuts
CAKE
  1 package Duncan Hines®
    Moist Deluxe Yellow
    Cake Mix
  1 can (16 ounces) solid
    pack pumpkin
  3 eggs
  ¼ cup butter or margarine,
    softened

1. Preheat oven to 350°F.

2. **For streusel,** combine brown sugar and cinnamon in small bowl. Cut in ⅓ cup butter with pastry blender or 2 knives. Stir in nuts; set aside.

3. **For cake,** combine cake mix, pumpkin, eggs and ¼ cup butter in large bowl. Beat at medium speed with electric mixer for 2 minutes. Spread half the batter into ungreased 13×9×2-inch pan. Sprinkle half the streusel over batter. Spread remaining batter over streusel. Top with remaining streusel. Bake at 350°F for 40 to 45 minutes or until toothpick inserted in center comes out clean.

Tip: Serve warm as a coffeecake or cool as a dessert topped with whipped topping.

Oatmeal Applesauce Squares

THANKSGIVING CRANBERRY COBBLER

9 Servings

2 cans (16 ounces each)
  sliced peaches in light
  syrup, drained
1 can (16 ounces) whole
  berry cranberry sauce
1 package Duncan Hines®
  Bakery Style
  Cinnamon Swirl
  Muffin Mix
½ cup chopped pecans
⅓ cup butter or margarine,
  melted
  Whipped topping or ice
  cream

1. Preheat oven to 350°F.

2. Cut peach slices in half lengthwise. Combine peach slices and cranberry sauce in ungreased 9-inch square pan. Knead swirl packet from Mix for 10 seconds. Cut off one end of packet. Squeeze contents evenly over fruit.

3. Combine muffin mix, contents of topping packet from Mix and pecans in large bowl. Add melted butter. Stir until thoroughly blended (mixture will be crumbly). Sprinkle crumbs over fruit. Bake at 350°F for 40 to 45 minutes or until lightly browned and bubbly. Serve warm with whipped topping.

Tip: Store shelled pecans in the refrigerator for up to 3 months or in the freezer for up to 6 months.

APPLE CUSTARD DESSERT

12 to 16 Servings

1 package Duncan Hines®
  Moist Deluxe Butter
  Recipe Golden
  Cake Mix
1 cup flaked coconut
½ cup butter or margarine,
  softened
6 medium apples, peeled,
  cored and thinly sliced
1 cup water
¼ cup lemon juice

1. Preheat oven to 350°F. Grease and flour 13×9×2-inch pan.

2. Combine cake mix and coconut in large bowl. Cut in butter with pastry blender or 2 knives. Arrange apple slices in pan. Sprinkle with crumb mixture. Combine water and lemon juice in 2-cup liquid measure. Pour evenly over top. Do not stir. Bake at 350°F for 45 to 50 minutes or until top is lightly browned and set. Cool slightly before serving.

Tip: Granny Smith, Golden Delicious, Rome Beauty, Winesap, McIntosh and Jonathan apple varieties all yield delicious results in this recipe.

Thanksgiving Cranberry Cobbler

CARAMEL PECAN SPICE CAKES

2 Loaves (24 Slices)

CAKE

1 package Duncan Hines®
   Moist Deluxe Spice
   Cake Mix
1 package (4-serving size)
   vanilla instant pudding
   and pie filling mix
4 eggs
1 cup water
⅓ cup Crisco® Oil or
   Crisco® Puritan® Oil
1½ cups pecan pieces,
   toasted and finely
   chopped (see Tip)

CARAMEL GLAZE

3 tablespoons butter or
   margarine
3 tablespoons granulated
   sugar
3 tablespoons brown
   sugar
3 tablespoons whipping
   cream
½ cup confectioners sugar
¼ teaspoon vanilla extract
   Pecan halves, for
   garnish
   Maraschino cherry
   halves, for garnish

1. Preheat oven to 350°F. Grease and flour two 8½×4½×2½-inch loaf pans.

2. **For cake,** combine cake mix, pudding mix, eggs, water and oil in large bowl. Beat at medium speed with electric mixer for 2 minutes. Stir in toasted pecans. Pour into pans. Bake at 350°F for 55 to 60 minutes or until toothpick inserted in center comes out clean. Cool in pans 15 minutes. Loosen loaves from pans. Invert onto cooling rack. Turn right-side up. Cool completely.

3. **For caramel glaze,** combine butter, granulated sugar, brown sugar and whipping cream in small heavy saucepan. Bring to a boil on medium heat; boil 1 minute. Remove from heat; cool 20 minutes. Add confectioners sugar and vanilla extract; blend with wooden spoon until smooth and thick. Spread evenly on cooled loaves. Garnish with pecan halves and maraschino cherry halves before glaze sets.

Tip: To toast pecans, spread pecan pieces evenly on baking sheet. Toast in 350°F oven for about 8 minutes or until fragrant. Cool completely.

Caramel Pecan Spice Cakes

BUTTERY CRANBERRY COBBLER

10 to 12 Servings

1 package Duncan Hines®
Moist Deluxe Butter
Recipe Golden Cake
Mix, divided
1 cup quick-cooking oats
(not instant or
old-fashioned)
¾ cup butter or margarine,
softened and divided
2 eggs
⅓ cup water
1 can (16 ounces) whole
berry cranberry sauce

1. Preheat oven to 375°F. Grease and flour 13×9×2-inch pan.

2. For topping, combine ½ cup cake mix, oats and ¼ cup butter in medium bowl with fork until crumbly. Set aside.

3. For base, place remaining cake mix in large bowl. Cut in remaining ½ cup butter with fork until crumbly. Stir in eggs and water until mixture is moistened. Spread in bottom of pan.

4. Stir cranberry sauce until smooth. Spread over batter in pan. Sprinkle with reserved topping. Bake at 375°F for 35 to 40 minutes or until toothpick inserted in center comes out clean. Cool 10 minutes before serving.

> **Tip:** To quickly soften cold butter, place 1 unwrapped stick of butter in microwave oven and microwave at HIGH (100% power) for 10 seconds.

ORANGE PECAN GEMS

4½ to 5 Dozen Cookies

1 package Duncan Hines®
Moist Deluxe Orange
Supreme Cake Mix
1 container (8 ounces)
vanilla lowfat yogurt
1 egg
2 tablespoons butter or
margarine, softened
1 cup finely chopped
pecans
1 cup pecan halves

1. Preheat oven to 350°F. Grease baking sheets.

2. Combine cake mix, yogurt, egg, butter and chopped pecans in large bowl. Beat at low speed with electric mixer until blended. Drop by rounded teaspoonfuls 2 inches apart onto baking sheets. Press pecan half onto center of each cookie. Bake at 350°F for 11 to 13 minutes or until golden brown. Cool 1 minute on baking sheets. Remove to cooling racks. Cool completely. Store in airtight container.

> **Tip:** Cookies may be stored in an airtight container in freezer for up to 6 months.

PUMPKIN SPICE CAKE WITH PUMPKIN CREAM TOPPING

12 to 16 Servings

CAKE
  1 package Duncan Hines®
    Moist Deluxe Spice
    Cake Mix
  2 eggs
  1 cup water
  1 can (16 ounces) solid
    pack pumpkin, divided
  1 cup chopped nuts
    Confectioners sugar

TOPPING
  1 container (8 ounces)
    frozen whipped
    topping, thawed
  1 tablespoon granulated
    sugar

1. Preheat oven to 350°F. Grease and flour 10-inch Bundt® pan.

2. **For cake,** combine cake mix, eggs, water and 1 cup pumpkin in large bowl. Beat at medium speed with electric mixer for 2 minutes. Stir in nuts. Pour into pan. Bake at 350°F for 40 to 50 minutes or until toothpick inserted in center comes out clean. Cool in pan 25 minutes. Invert onto serving plate. Cool completely. Dust with confectioners sugar.

3. **For topping,** mix together whipped topping, remaining ¾ cup pumpkin and granulated sugar. Spoon over cake slices to serve.

> **Tip:** To dust cake easily, place confectioners sugar in a small strainer and gently shake over cake.

APPLESAUCE WALNUT CAKE

12 to 16 Servings

  1 package Duncan Hines®
    Moist Deluxe Butter
    Recipe Golden
    Cake Mix
  3 eggs
  1⅓ cups applesauce
  ½ cup butter or margarine,
    melted
  1 teaspoon ground
    cinnamon
  ½ cup chopped walnuts
    Confectioners sugar

1. Preheat oven to 375°F. Grease and flour 10-inch Bundt® or tube pan.

2. Combine cake mix, eggs, applesauce, melted butter and cinnamon in large bowl. Beat at low speed with electric mixer until moistened. Beat at medium speed for 4 minutes. Stir in walnuts. Pour into pan. Bake at 375°F for 45 to 55 minutes or until toothpick inserted in center comes out clean. Cool in pan 25 minutes. Invert cake onto serving plate. Cool completely. Dust with confectioners sugar.

> **Tip:** Also delicious using chopped pecans instead of walnuts.

12 to 16 Servings

CRUST
**1 package Duncan Hines®
Moist Deluxe Spice
Cake Mix**
**½ cup Crisco® Oil or
Crisco® Puritan® Oil**
½ teaspoon salt
¼ teaspoon baking soda

TOPPING
**1 can (16 ounces) solid
pack pumpkin**
**1 can (12 ounces)
evaporated milk**
2 eggs, lightly beaten
¾ cup sugar
**1 teaspoon ground
cinnamon**
½ teaspoon salt
½ teaspoon ground ginger
¼ teaspoon ground cloves
**Whipped topping, for
garnish**
**Pecan halves, for
garnish**

1. Preheat oven to 350°F.

2. **For crust,** combine cake mix, oil, ½ teaspoon salt and baking soda in large bowl. Stir until thoroughly blended. Spread evenly in ungreased 13×9×2-inch pan. Bake at 350°F for 20 to 25 minutes or until set.

3. **For topping,** combine pumpkin, evaporated milk, eggs, sugar, cinnamon, ½ teaspoon salt, ginger and cloves in large bowl. Stir to blend well. Pour pumpkin mixture over hot crust. Bake at 350°F for 25 to 30 minutes or until center is firm. Cool completely. Refrigerate until ready to serve. Cut into squares. Garnish with dollops of whipped topping. Decorate with pecan halves.

Tip: For a different presentation serve with ice cream and garnish with shaved chocolate.

Pumpkin Squares

12 to 16 Servings

CAKE
  1 package Duncan Hines®
     Moist Deluxe Yellow
     Cake Mix
  3 eggs
  1¼ cups apple juice
  ⅓ cup Crisco® Oil or
     Crisco® Puritan® Oil
  1 teaspoon ground
     cinnamon
  2 cups peeled, grated
     apples (about
     2 medium)
  ½ cup all-purpose flour
  1 cup chopped pecans

FROSTING
  3 tablespoons butter or
     margarine
  3 tablespoons granulated
     sugar
  3 tablespoons brown
     sugar
  3 tablespoons whipping
     cream
  ½ cup confectioners sugar
  ¼ teaspoon vanilla extract
     Pecan halves, for
     garnish

1. Preheat oven to 350°F. Grease and flour 10-inch tube pan.

2. **For cake,** combine cake mix, eggs, apple juice, oil and cinnamon in large bowl. Beat at medium speed with electric mixer for 2 minutes. Toss apples with flour in medium bowl. Fold flour-coated apples and chopped pecans into batter. Pour into pan. Bake at 350°F for 45 minutes or until toothpick inserted in center comes out clean. Cool in pan 25 minutes. Invert onto serving plate. Cool completely.

3. **For frosting,** combine butter, granulated sugar, brown sugar and whipping cream in small heavy saucepan. Bring to a boil over medium heat; boil 1 minute. Remove from heat; cool 20 minutes. Add confectioners sugar and vanilla extract; blend with wooden spoon until smooth and thick. Spread frosting on cake. Garnish with pecan halves.

Tip: Apples may be grated in a food processor using the shredding disc. If a food processor is not available, use a hand grater.

Fresh Apple Cake

LEMON CRANBERRY LOAVES

2 Loaves (24 Slices)

1¼ cups finely chopped
    fresh cranberries
½ cup finely chopped
    walnuts
¼ cup granulated sugar
1 package Duncan Hines®
    Moist Deluxe Lemon
    Supreme Cake Mix
1 package (3 ounces)
    cream cheese, softened
¾ cup milk
4 eggs
    Confectioners sugar

1. Preheat oven to 350°F. Grease and flour two 8½×4½×2½-inch loaf pans.

2. Stir together cranberries, walnuts and granulated sugar in large bowl; set aside.

3. Combine cake mix, cream cheese and milk in large bowl. Beat at medium speed with electric mixer for 2 minutes. Add eggs, one at a time, beating well after each addition. Fold in cranberry mixture. Pour into pans. Bake at 350°F for 45 to 50 minutes or until toothpick inserted in center comes out clean. Cool in pans 15 minutes. Loosen loaves from pans. Invert onto cooling rack. Turn right-side up. Cool completely. Dust with confectioners sugar.

> **Tip:** To quickly chop cranberries or walnuts, use a food processor.

APPLE NUT POUND CAKE

12 to 16 Servings

1 package Duncan Hines®
    Moist Deluxe Yellow
    Cake Mix
1 package (4-serving size)
    vanilla instant pudding
    and pie filling mix
2 teaspoons cinnamon
4 eggs
1 cup applesauce
1 cup raisins
1 cup chopped pecans
⅔ cup Crisco® Oil or
    Crisco® Puritan® Oil
¼ cup chopped maraschino
    cherries
    Confectioners sugar

1. Preheat oven to 350°F. Grease and flour 10-inch Bundt® pan.

2. Combine cake mix, pudding mix and cinnamon in large bowl. Add remaining ingredients except confectioners sugar; stir with wooden spoon. Pour into pan. Bake at 350°F for 50 to 55 minutes or until toothpick inserted in center comes out clean. Cool in pan 25 minutes. Invert onto serving plate. Cool completely. Dust with confectioners sugar.

> **Tip:** For an enhanced flavor, toast the pecans before adding to cake batter. Bake pecans in a single layer on baking sheet at 325°F for 3 to 5 minutes.

Lemon Cranberry Loaf

PUMPKIN PIE CRUNCH

16 to 20 Servings

1 can (16 ounces) solid pack pumpkin
1 can (12 ounces) evaporated milk
3 eggs
1½ cups sugar
4 teaspoons pumpkin pie spice
½ teaspoon salt
1 package Duncan Hines® Moist Deluxe Yellow Cake Mix
1 cup chopped pecans
1 cup butter or margarine, melted
Whipped topping

1. Preheat oven to 350°F. Grease bottom of 13×9×2-inch pan.

2. Combine pumpkin, evaporated milk, eggs, sugar, pumpkin pie spice and salt in large bowl. Pour into pan. Sprinkle cake mix evenly over pumpkin mixture. Top with pecans. Drizzle with melted butter. Bake at 350°F for 50 to 55 minutes or until golden. Cool completely. Cut into squares. Serve with whipped topping. Refrigerate leftovers.

Tip: For a richer flavor, try using Duncan Hines® Moist Deluxe Butter Recipe Golden Cake Mix.

CRANBERRY STRAWBERRY CAKE

16 to 20 Servings

1 package Duncan Hines® Moist Deluxe Strawberry Supreme Cake Mix
1 container (12 ounces) cranberry-strawberry sauce
1 container (8 ounces) frozen whipped topping, thawed

1. Preheat oven to 350°F. Grease and flour 13×9×2-inch pan.

2. Prepare, bake and cool cake following package directions for original recipe.

3. Spread cranberry-strawberry sauce on top of cake. Frost with whipped topping. Refrigerate until ready to serve.

Tip: Garnish each serving with a fresh strawberry, if desired.

Pumpkin Pie Crunch

Festive Desserts

TRIPLE CHOCOLATE FANTASY

12 to 16 Servings

CAKE
  **1 package Duncan Hines®
    Moist Deluxe Devil's
    Food Cake Mix**
  3 eggs
  1⅓ cups water
  **½ cup Crisco® Oil or
    Crisco® Puritan® Oil**
  **½ cup ground walnuts
    (see Tip)**
CHOCOLATE GLAZE
  **1 package (12 ounces)
    semi-sweet chocolate
    chips**
  **¼ cup *plus* 2 tablespoons
    butter or margarine**
  **¼ cup coarsely chopped
    walnuts, for garnish**
**WHITE CHOCOLATE
GLAZE**
  **3 ounces white chocolate,
    coarsely chopped**
  **1 tablespoon Crisco®
    Shortening**

1. Preheat oven to 350°F. Grease and flour 10-inch Bundt® pan.

2. **For cake,** combine cake mix, eggs, water, oil and ground walnuts in large bowl. Beat at medium speed with electric mixer for 2 minutes. Pour into pan. Bake at 350°F for 45 to 55 minutes or until toothpick inserted in center comes out clean. Cool in pan 25 minutes. Invert onto serving plate. Cool completely.

3. **For chocolate glaze,** combine chocolate chips and butter in small heavy saucepan. Heat over low heat until chips are melted. Stir constantly until shiny and smooth. (Glaze will be very thick.) Spread hot glaze over cooled cake. Garnish with chopped walnuts.

4. **For white chocolate glaze,** combine white chocolate and shortening in small heavy saucepan. Heat on low heat until melted, stirring constantly. Drizzle hot glaze over top of cake.

Tip: To grind walnuts, use food processor fitted with steel blade.
Process until fine.

Triple Chocolate Fantasy

RASPBERRY ALMOND
SANDWICH COOKIES

4½ to 5 Dozen Sandwich Cookies

**1 package Duncan Hines®
  Golden Sugar
  Cookie Mix**
1 egg
1 tablespoon water
½ teaspoon almond extract
**¾ cup sliced natural
  almonds, broken
  Seedless red raspberry
  jam**

1. Preheat oven to 375°F.

2. Combine cookie mix, contents of buttery flavor packet from Mix, egg, water and almond extract in large bowl. Stir until thoroughly blended. Drop half the dough by level measuring teaspoonfuls 2 inches apart onto ungreased baking sheets. (It is a small amount of dough but will spread during baking to 1½ to 1¾ inches.)

3. Place almonds on waxed paper. Drop other half of dough by level measuring teaspoons onto almonds. Place almond-side up 2 inches apart on baking sheets.

4. Bake both plain cookies and almond cookies at 375°F for 6 minutes or until set but not browned. Cool 1 minute on baking sheets. Remove to cooling racks. Cool completely.

5. Spread bottoms of plain cookies with jam; top with almond cookies. Press together to make sandwiches. Store in airtight container.

Tip: For a delicious variation, fill with Duncan Hines® Milk Chocolate Frosting instead of raspberry jam.

Raspberry Almond Sandwich Cookies

CHOCOLATE CHERRY CHEESECAKE

12 to 16 Servings

CRUST
  1 package Duncan Hines®
    Fudge Brownie Mix,
    Family Size, divided
  2 tablespoons butter or
    margarine, softened
  1 teaspoon water

FILLING
  3 packages (8 ounces
    each) cream cheese,
    softened
  ¾ cup sugar
  2 tablespoons all-purpose
    flour
  3 eggs, lightly beaten
  2 tablespoons lemon juice
  1 teaspoon vanilla extract
  1 can (21 ounces) cherry
    pie filling

1. Preheat oven to 350°F.

2. Reserve 2½ cups brownie mix for Brownies (see recipe below).

3. **For crust,** place remaining brownie mix in medium bowl. Cut in butter with pastry blender or 2 knives until mixture is crumbly. Stir in water. Pat mixture into bottom of ungreased 9-inch springform pan. Bake at 350°F for 10 to 12 minutes or until set. Remove from oven. *Increase oven temperature to 450°F.*

4. **For filling,** place cream cheese in large bowl. Beat at low speed with electric mixer adding sugar and flour gradually. Add eggs, lemon juice and vanilla extract, mixing only until incorporated. Pour filling onto crust. Bake at 450°F for 10 minutes. *Reduce oven temperature to 250°F.* Bake for 28 to 33 minutes longer or until cheesecake is set. Loosen cake from sides of pan with knife or spatula. Cool completely on rack. Remove sides of pan. Spoon cherry pie filling over top. Refrigerate 2 hours or until ready to serve.

BROWNIES

9 to 12 Brownies

  2½ cups reserved
    brownie mix
  1 egg
  ¼ cup Crisco® Oil or
    Crisco® Puritan® Oil
  3 tablespoons water

Preheat oven to 350°F. Grease bottom of 8-inch square pan. Combine reserved brownie mix, egg, oil and water in medium bowl. Stir with spoon until well blended, about 50 strokes. Spread in pan. Bake at 350°F for about 25 minutes or until set. Cool completely. Cut into bars.

Tip: Prepare the Chocolate Cherry Cheesecake for company and the Brownies for your children.

Chocolate Cherry Cheesecake

CHRISTMAS TREE CAKE

16 to 20 Servings

1 package Duncan Hines®
    Moist Deluxe Cake
    Mix (any flavor)

FROSTING
 5 cups confectioners sugar
 ¾ cup Crisco® Shortening
 ½ cup water
 ⅓ cup non-dairy powdered
    creamer
 2 teaspoons vanilla
    extract
 ½ teaspoon salt
 1 tablespoon green food
    coloring
    Peppermint candies
    Pretzel rods
    Large gumdrops

1. Preheat oven to 350°F. Grease and flour 13×9×2-inch pan.

2. Prepare, bake and cool cake following package directions for original recipe.

3. **For frosting,** combine confectioners sugar, shortening, water, non-dairy powdered creamer, vanilla extract and salt in large bowl. Beat at medium speed with electric mixer for 3 minutes. Beat at high speed for 5 minutes. Add more confectioners sugar to thicken or more water to thin as needed. Reserve 1 cup frosting. Tint remaining frosting with green food coloring.

4. Cut cooled cake and arrange as shown. Spread green frosting over cake. Decorate tree with reserved white frosting and peppermint candies. Make tree trunk of pretzel rods. Roll out large gumdrop and cut with star cookie cutter. Top tree with gumdrop star.

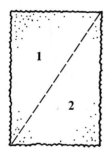 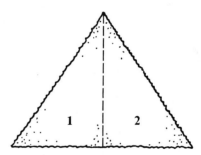

Tip: To make the garland, pipe frosting using a pastry bag fitted with a star tip, or use red lace licorice.

Christmas Tree Cake

20 Petits Fours

**1 package Duncan Hines®
   Moist Deluxe White or
   Yellow Cake Mix**

ICING
 3 cups granulated sugar
 1½ cups hot water
 ¼ teaspoon cream of tartar
 1 teaspoon vanilla extract
 **2¼ cups confectioners sugar
   Food coloring (optional)
   Decorator frosting and
   assorted decors
   (optional)**

1. Preheat oven to 350°F. Line 15½×10½×1-inch jelly-roll pan with waxed paper.

2. Prepare cake following package directions for original recipe. Pour into pan. Bake at 350°F for 25 minutes or until toothpick inserted in center comes out clean. Invert cake onto large baking sheet. Remove waxed paper. Cool completely. Cut cake into 20 pieces, approximately 3×2½ inches each. Place cakes on cooling racks with waxed paper under racks.

3. **For icing,** combine granulated sugar, hot water and cream of tartar in heavy saucepan. Cook until mixture reaches 220°F on a candy thermometer. Cook at 220°F until syrup spins a thread. Cool until lukewarm or 110°F. Stir in vanilla extract. Beat in confectioners sugar gradually until icing is a good pouring consistency. Divide icing into small bowls. Tint icing in each bowl with 3 to 4 drops food coloring, if desired.

4. Pour icing over cakes. Remove spilled icing from waxed paper and return to icing bowl. Reheat icing over hot water if icing becomes too thick. Decorate with additional frosting and assorted decors, if desired.

Tip: Personalize your petits fours! For instance, if the mother-to-be has chosen names, decorate each petit four with a letter and spell out the names.

Baby Shower Petits Fours

SUGAR COOKIE WREATHS

2 Dozen Cookies

1 package Duncan Hines®
  Golden Sugar
  Cookie Mix
1 egg
  Green food coloring
  Candied or maraschino
  cherry pieces

1. Preheat oven to 375°F.

2. Combine cookie mix, contents of buttery flavor packet from Mix and egg in large bowl. Stir until thoroughly blended.

3. Tint dough with green food coloring. Stir until desired color. Form into balls the size of miniature marshmallows. For each wreath, arrange 9 or 10 balls with sides touching into a ring. Place wreaths 2 inches apart on ungreased baking sheets. Flatten slightly with fingers. Place small piece of candied cherry on each ball.

4. Bake at 375°F for 5 to 7 minutes or until set but not browned. Cool 1 minute on baking sheets. Remove to cooling racks. Cool completely. Store in airtight container.

Note: If using maraschino cherries, drain well after chopping into pieces.

> **Tip:** Instead of tinting dough green, coat balls with green sugar crystals.

GRASSHOPPER DESSERT

12 Servings

CRUST
  1 package Duncan Hines®
    Moist Deluxe Dark
    Dutch Fudge Cake
    Mix, divided
1 egg
½ cup butter or margarine,
  softened

1. Preheat oven to 350°F. Grease and flour 13×9×2-inch pan. Remove ½ cup cake mix and spread in 8-inch ungreased baking pan. Toast in oven for 7 minutes. Cool.

2. **For crust,** combine remaining cake mix, egg and butter in large bowl. Mix until crumbs form. Press lightly into prepared 13×9×2-inch pan. Bake at 350°F for 15 minutes. Cool.

(continued)

FILLING

3 cups miniature
marshmallows
½ cup milk
⅓ cup green creme de
menthe
2 tablespoons white creme
de cacao
1½ cups whipping cream,
chilled

3. **For filling,** heat marshmallows and milk in medium saucepan over low heat. Stir constantly until marshmallows melt. Refrigerate until thickened. Stir creme de menthe and creme de cacao into marshmallow mixture.

4. Beat whipping cream until stiff in large bowl. Fold in marshmallow mixture. Pour into crust. Dust top with cooled toasted dry mix. Refrigerate until ready to serve. Cut into squares.

Tip: To quickly chill marshmallow mixture, pour mixture into medium bowl; place in larger bowl of ice water and refrigerate. Stir occasionally.

CREAMY EGGNOG DESSERT

12 to 16 Servings

CRUST

1 package Duncan Hines®
Moist Deluxe Swiss
Chocolate Cake Mix
½ cup butter or margarine,
melted
½ cup chopped pecans

FILLING

1 package (8 ounces)
cream cheese, softened
1 cup sugar
1 container (12 ounces)
frozen whipped
topping, thawed and
divided
2 packages (4-serving size
each) French vanilla
instant pudding and
pie filling mix
3 cups cold milk
¼ teaspoon rum extract
¼ teaspoon ground nutmeg

1. Preheat oven to 350°F.

2. **For crust,** combine cake mix, melted butter and pecans. Reserve ½ cup mixture. Press remaining mixture into bottom of ungreased 13×9×2-inch pan. Bake at 350°F for 15 to 20 minutes or until surface is firm. Cool. Toast reserved mixture on cookie sheet at 350°F for 3 to 4 minutes, stirring once. Cool completely. Break up any lumps with fork to make small crumbs. Set aside.

3. **For filling,** beat cream cheese and sugar until smooth in large bowl. Stir in 1 cup whipped topping. Spread over cooled crust. Refrigerate. Combine pudding mix and milk. Beat 1 minute. Add rum extract and nutmeg. Spread over cheese layer. Spread remaining whipped topping over pudding layer. Sprinkle with reserved toasted mixture. Refrigerate at least 2 hours.

Tip: For successful baking, using the correct measuring cup is important. A lipped measuring cup is for measuring liquids and a flush rimmed cup is for measuring dry ingredients.

12 to 16 Servings

1 package Duncan Hines®
  Moist Deluxe White
  Cake Mix
  Green and red food
  coloring
1 container (16 ounces)
  Duncan Hines® Cream
  Cheese Layer Cake
  Frosting, divided
½ cup strawberry jam
½ cup semi-sweet
  chocolate chips or mini
  chocolate chips

1. Preheat oven to 350°F. Grease and flour two 9-inch round cake pans.

2. Cut two aluminum foil pieces 24 inches long. Fold and refold until each strip is 2 inches wide. Mold strips around 7-inch round bowl to shape. Tape ends together to form two 7-inch circles.

3. Prepare cake following package directions for original recipe. Measure 1½ cups batter into bowl. Add 12 drops green food coloring. Add 15 drops red food coloring to remaining batter. Stir until thoroughly blended. Place foil circles in center of pans. Pour half the pink batter inside each foil circle. Pour half the green batter outside each foil circle. Pull out foil. Bake and cool cake following package directions.

4. Tint ½ cup Cream Cheese frosting to desired pink color. Tint remaining frosting to desired green color.

5. To assemble, place one cake layer on serving plate. Spread jam on pink area of cake layer. Spread green frosting on green part of cake layer. Top with second cake layer. Frost sides and green area on top layer with green frosting. Spread pink frosting on center of cake top; sprinkle with chocolate chips.

Tip: Create your own special cake color combinations by tinting batter with different food colorings.

Watermelon Cake

PEANUT BUTTER REINDEER

About 2 Dozen Cookies

COOKIES
  1 package Duncan Hines®
    Peanut Butter
    Cookie Mix
  1 egg
  2 teaspoons all-purpose
    flour

ASSORTED DECORATIONS
  Semi-sweet mini
    chocolate chips
  Vanilla milk chips
  Candy-coated semi-
    sweet chocolate chips
  Colored sprinkles

1. **For cookies,** combine cookie mix, contents of peanut butter packet from Mix and egg in large bowl. Stir until thoroughly blended. Form dough into ball. Place flour in jumbo (15×13-inch) resealable plastic bag. Place ball of dough in bag. Shake to coat with flour. Place dough in center of bag (do not seal). Roll dough with rolling pin out to edges of bag. Slide bag onto baking sheet. Chill in refrigerator at least 1 hour.

2. Preheat oven to 375°F.

3. Use scissors to cut bag down center and across ends. Turn plastic back to uncover dough. Dip reindeer cookie cutter in flour. Cut dough with reindeer cookie cutter. Dip cookie cutter in flour after each cut. Transfer cutout cookies using floured pancake turner to ungreased baking sheets. Decorate as desired making eyes, mouth, nose and tail with assorted decorations. Bake at 375°F for 5 to 7 minutes or until set but not browned. Cool 2 minutes on baking sheets. Remove to cooling racks. Cool completely. Store between layers of waxed paper in airtight container.

Tips: Reroll dough by folding plastic back over dough.
To use as ornaments, press end of drinking straw in top of each cookie
before baking. Press straw through cookies again after baking. String
ribbon through holes of cooled cookies. Tie at top.

Peanut Butter Reindeer

ALL-OCCASION NUMBER CAKE

12 to 16 Servings

1 package Duncan Hines® Moist Deluxe Cake Mix (any flavor)
4 cups confectioners sugar
½ cup unsweetened cocoa
¾ cup Crisco® Shortening
¼ cup hot water, divided
2 tablespoons light corn syrup
1 teaspoon vanilla extract
1 container (16 ounces) Duncan Hines® Vanilla Layer Cake Frosting

1. Preheat oven to 350°F. Grease and flour 13×9×2-inch pan.

2. Prepare, bake and cool cake following package directions for original recipe. Remove from pan. Freeze cake for ease in handling.

3. To make numbers, trim ¼ to ½ inch from edges of frozen cake. Cut cake into 2 equal portions. Cut each cake portion into desired number using sharp knife. Follow number chart below as guide.

4. For chocolate frosting, combine confectioners sugar, cocoa and shortening in large bowl. Add 2 tablespoons hot water and beat until smooth. Add corn syrup, vanilla extract and remaining 2 tablespoons hot water. Beat until smooth and creamy. Add more confectioners sugar to thicken or water to thin frosting as needed. Spread chocolate frosting on sides and top of cakes. Place star tip in decorating bag. Fill with Vanilla frosting. Decorate as desired.

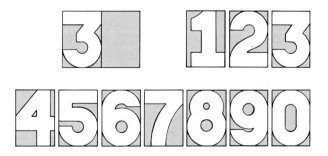

Tip: Cakes are easier to frost when completely frozen. After cutting into desired numbers, return to freezer while preparing frosting.

All-Occasion Number Cake

PINK PEPPERMINT SURPRISE

12 to 16 Servings

1 teaspoon peppermint
   extract
6 to 8 drops red food
   coloring
1 package Duncan Hines®
   Angel Food Cake Mix
½ gallon vanilla ice cream
½ cup chocolate fudge ice
   cream topping
   Peppermint candies,
   crushed

1. Preheat oven to 375°F.

2. Add peppermint extract and 6 to 8 drops food coloring to egg white packet from Mix and water in large bowl. Prepare, bake and cool cake following package directions.

3. Serve each cake slice with vanilla ice cream, chocolate fudge ice cream topping and crushed peppermint candy.

Tip: For a flavor variation, serve with mint chocolate chip ice cream instead of vanilla.

CHERRY CHOCOLATE CHIP COOKIES

3½ to 4 Dozen Cookies

1 package Duncan Hines®
   Moist Deluxe Yellow
   Cake Mix
½ cup butter or margarine,
   melted
1 egg
1 package (6 ounces)
   semi-sweet chocolate
   chips
½ cup chopped pecans
¼ cup chopped maraschino
   cherries, drained

1. Preheat oven to 375°F.

2. Combine cake mix, melted butter and egg in large bowl. Stir in chocolate chips, pecans and maraschino cherries.

3. Drop by slightly rounded teaspoonfuls onto ungreased baking sheets. Bake at 375°F for 10 to 12 minutes or until lightly browned. Cool 1 minute on baking sheets. Remove to cooling racks. Cool completely. Store in airtight container.

Tip: For a festive holiday appearance, use both red *and* green maraschino cherries.

Pink Peppermint Surprise

CHERRY PINEAPPLE TRIFLE

24 Large or 32 Small Servings

1 package Duncan Hines®
  Moist Deluxe Yellow
  Cake Mix
1 package (4-serving size)
  vanilla instant pudding
  and pie filling mix
2 cups chopped pecans
1 can (15¼ ounces)
  crushed pineapple,
  drained
1 can (21 ounces) cherry
  pie filling
1 package (12 ounces)
  flaked coconut
  (3½ cups)
2 containers (8 ounces
  each) frozen whipped
  topping, thawed

1. Preheat oven to 350°F. Grease and flour two 9-inch round cake pans.

2. Prepare, bake and cool cake following package directions for original recipe.

3. Prepare instant pudding following package directions. Refrigerate until ready to use.

4. Reserve ¼ cup chopped pecans. Crumble one cake layer in 6-quart trifle dish. Layer half each of pudding, pineapple, cherry pie filling, coconut, remaining pecans and whipped topping. Repeat layers, beginning with crumbling second cake layer. Top with reserved pecans. Refrigerate until ready to serve.

Tip: If a trifle dish is not available, use a 6-quart clear glass bowl with straight sides.

RICH DOUBLE CHOCOLATE CREAM TORTE

8 to 12 Servings

BROWNIE
1 package Duncan Hines®
  Brownies Plus Milk
  Chocolate Chunks
  Brownie Mix
3 eggs
⅓ cup water
⅓ cup Crisco® Oil or
  Crisco® Puritan® Oil
½ cup finely chopped nuts

1. Preheat oven to 350°F. Grease and flour 9-inch round pan.

2. **For brownie,** combine brownie mix, eggs, water, oil and nuts. Stir with spoon until well blended, about 50 strokes. Pour into pan. Bake at 350°F for 35 to 40 minutes. Cool 30 minutes in pan. Run knife along edge of pan. Invert onto serving platter.

(continued)

CHOCOLATE BUTTERCREAM

1 package (6 ounces) semi-sweet chocolate chips, melted
½ cup butter or margarine, softened
2 tablespoons whipping cream

WHIPPED CREAM

¾ cup *plus* 2 tablespoons whipping cream, chilled
2 tablespoons sugar
1 tablespoon colored sprinkles

3. **For chocolate buttercream,** stir together melted chocolate, butter and 2 tablespoons whipping cream. Spread over top of brownie.

4. **For whipped cream,** beat ¾ cup *plus* 2 tablespoons whipping cream and sugar at high speed with electric mixer for 1 to 3 minutes or until thick. Spread over chocolate buttercream. Sprinkle with colored sprinkles. Refrigerate until ready to serve.

Note: One half pint whipping cream will yield enough whipping cream for this recipe.

Tips: Chilling the beaters and bowl before whipping the cream decreases whipping time and helps insure good volume.

EASTER BASKET CUPCAKES

24 Cupcakes

1 package Duncan Hines® Moist Deluxe Yellow Cake Mix
3 tablespoons *plus* 1½ teaspoons water
6 drops green food coloring
1½ cups shredded coconut
1 container (16 ounces) Duncan Hines® Vanilla Layer Cake Frosting
½ pound assorted colored jelly beans
24 assorted colored pipe cleaners

1. Preheat oven to 350°F. Place 2½-inch paper liners in 24 muffin cups.

2. Prepare, bake and cool cupcakes following package directions for original recipe.

3. Combine water and food coloring in large container with tight fitting lid. Add coconut. Shake until coconut is evenly tinted green.

4. Frost cupcakes with Vanilla frosting. Sprinkle coconut over frosting. Press 3 jelly beans into coconut on each cupcake. Bend pipe cleaners to form basket handles. Push into cupcakes.

Tip: You can make fruit baskets by placing fruit slices on top of frosting in place of coconut and jelly beans.

CANDY CANE CAKE

12 to 16 Servings

**1 package Duncan Hines®
Moist Deluxe Cake
Mix (any flavor)**

FROSTING
5 cups confectioners sugar
¾ cup Crisco® Shortening
½ cup water
**⅓ cup non-dairy powdered
creamer**
**2 teaspoons vanilla
extract**
½ teaspoon salt
Red food coloring
**Maraschino cherry
halves, well drained**

1. Preheat oven to 350°F. Grease and flour 13×9×2-inch pan.

2. Prepare, bake and cool cake following package directions for original recipe. Remove from pan. Freeze cake for ease in handling.

3. **For frosting,** combine confectioners sugar, shortening, water, non-dairy powdered creamer, vanilla extract and salt in large bowl. Beat at medium speed with electric mixer for 3 minutes. Beat at high speed for 5 minutes. Add more confectioners sugar to thicken or water to thin frosting as needed. Reserve 2 cups frosting. Tint remaining frosting with red food coloring.

4. Cut frozen cake and arrange as shown. Spread white frosting on cake. Mark candy cane stripes in frosting with tip of knife. Place star tip in decorating bag and fill with red frosting. To make stripes, arrange maraschino cherry halves and pipe red frosting following lines.

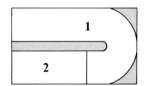 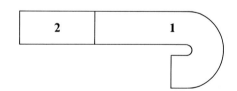

Tip: For a quick dessert, serve leftover cake pieces with sugared strawberries or dollops of whipped cream.

Candy Cane Cake

APRIL FOOL SURPRISE CAKE

12 to 16 Servings

CAKE
  **1 package Duncan Hines®
    Moist Deluxe Fudge
    Marble Cake Mix**
  3 eggs
  1¼ cups water
  **⅓ cup Crisco® Oil or
    Crisco® Puritan® Oil**

FROSTING
  4 cups confectioners sugar
  **½ cup butter or margarine,
    softened**
  **2 squares (2 ounces)
    unsweetened chocolate,
    melted**
  ¼ cup water
  **1½ teaspoons vanilla
    extract**
  ¼ teaspoon salt
  **¼ cup apricot preserves,
    warmed**

1. Preheat oven to 350°F. Grease and flour two 9-inch round cake pans.

2. **For cake,** combine cake mix, eggs, 1¼ cups water and oil in large bowl. Beat at medium speed with electric mixer for 2 minutes. Pour half the batter into small bowl. Stir in contents of cocoa packet from Mix. Pour yellow batter into one cake pan. Pour chocolate batter into second cake pan. Bake at 350°F for 30 to 35 minutes or until toothpick inserted in center comes out clean. Cool cakes following package directions.

3. **For frosting,** combine confectioners sugar, butter, melted chocolate, ¼ cup water, vanilla extract and salt in large bowl. Beat at medium speed with electric mixer for 3 minutes. Beat at high speed for 3 to 5 minutes.

4. To assemble cake, cut cardboard circle into size of cake layer. Cut out center of circle leaving 1½-inch rim. Place cardboard rim on cake layer. Cut out cake center with sharp knife. Repeat for second cake layer. Remove centers. Spread all cut edges of centers with warmed preserves. Place yellow cake rim on serving plate. Insert chocolate cake center into yellow cake rim. Spread with frosting. Place chocolate cake rim on top of first layer. Insert yellow cake center into chocolate cake rim. Frost sides and top with frosting.

Tip: For an additional topping, melt ¼ cup semi-sweet chocolate chips; drizzle on top of cake.

April Fool Surprise Cake

GLAZED SUGAR COOKIES

2½ to 3 Dozen Cookies

COOKIES
   **1 package Duncan Hines®
      Golden Sugar
      Cookie Mix**
   1 egg
GLAZE
   **1 cup sifted confectioners
      sugar**
   **1 to 2 tablespoons water
      or milk**
   **½ teaspoon vanilla extract
      Food coloring (optional)
      Red and green sugar
      crystals or decors**

1. Preheat oven to 375°F.

2. **For cookies,** combine cookie mix, contents of buttery flavor packet from Mix and egg in large bowl. Stir until thoroughly blended. Roll dough to ⅛-inch thickness on lightly floured surface. Cut dough into desired shapes using floured cookie cutters. Place cookies 2 inches apart on ungreased baking sheets. Bake at 375°F for 5 to 6 minutes or until edges are light golden brown. Cool 1 minute on baking sheets. Remove to cooling racks. Cool completely.

3. **For glaze,** combine confectioners sugar, water and vanilla extract in small bowl. Beat until smooth. Tint glaze with food coloring, if desired. Brush glaze on each cookie with clean pastry brush. Sprinkle cookies with sugar crystals or decors before glaze sets or decorate as desired. Allow glaze to set before storing between layers of waxed paper in airtight container.

Tip: Use Duncan Hines® Vanilla Frosting for a quick glaze. Heat frosting in opened container in microwave at HIGH (100% power) for 10 to 15 seconds. Stir well. Spread on cookies and decorate as desired before frosting sets.

Glazed Sugar Cookies

DOUBLE WEDDING RING CAKE

16 to 20 Servings

CAKE

  1 package Duncan Hines®
    Moist Deluxe Yellow
    Cake Mix
  1 package (4-serving size)
    vanilla instant pudding
    and pie filling mix
  4 eggs
  1 cup water
  ⅓ cup Crisco® Oil or
    Crisco® Puritan® Oil

FROSTING

  5 cups confectioners sugar
  ¾ cup Crisco® Shortening
  ½ cup water
  ⅓ cup non-dairy powdered
    creamer
  2 teaspoons vanilla
    extract
  ½ teaspoon salt

1. Preheat oven to 350°F. Grease generously and flour 10-inch tube pan.

2. **For cake,** combine cake mix, pudding mix, eggs, 1 cup water and oil in large bowl. Beat at medium speed with electric mixer for 2 minutes. Pour into pan. Bake at 350°F for 50 to 60 minutes or until toothpick inserted in center comes out clean. Cool cake in pan 25 minutes. Invert onto cooling rack. Cool completely. Split cake in half horizontally. Place cakes side-by-side and touching on large serving tray.

3. **For frosting,** combine confectioners sugar, shortening, ½ cup water, non-dairy powdered creamer, vanilla extract and salt in large mixing bowl. Beat at medium speed with electric mixer for 3 minutes. Beat at high speed for 5 minutes. Add more confectioners sugar to thicken or water to thin frosting as needed. Frost cake, reserving some frosting to decorate as desired with decorating set. Garnish with non-toxic flowers (see Tip page 25) or wedding decorations.

Tip: If decorator set is not available, roll up a 15-inch triangle of parchment paper and snip off the tip. Fill with frosting to pipe decorations on cake.

Double Wedding Ring Cake

BROWNIE HOLIDAY DESSERT

12 Servings

BROWNIE LAYERS
  **1 package Duncan Hines®
    Brownies Plus Milk
    Chocolate Chunks
    Mix**
  3 eggs
  ⅓ cup water
  **⅓ cup Crisco® Oil or
    Crisco® Puritan® Oil**

FILLING and FROSTING
  **1 package (4-serving size)
    French vanilla instant
    pudding and pie
    filling mix**
  ¼ cup confectioners sugar
  1 cup milk
  **1 container (8 ounces)
    frozen whipped
    topping, thawed**
  **1 can (8 ounces) pineapple
    tidbits, drained and
    divided**
  **¼ cup miniature
    marshmallows**
  ¼ cup flaked coconut
  **2 tablespoons chopped
    maraschino cherries**
  **Additional maraschino
    cherries, for garnish**

1. Preheat oven to 350°F. Grease two 8-inch round cake pans. Line with waxed paper.

2. **For brownie layers,** combine brownie mix, eggs, water and oil in large bowl. Stir with spoon until well blended, about 50 strokes. Pour into pans. Bake at 350°F for 25 to 30 minutes or until set. Cool in pans 15 minutes. Remove from pans. Peel waxed paper from bottoms. Cool completely.

3. **For filling and frosting,** combine pudding mix, confectioners sugar and milk in large bowl. Beat at low speed with electric mixer for 1 minute until well blended. Fold in whipped topping. Remove 1 cup mixture to small bowl. Stir in ⅓ cup pineapple, marshmallows, coconut and 2 tablespoons chopped cherries.

4. To assemble, place one brownie layer on serving plate. Spread with fruit filling. Top with second brownie layer. Frost sides and top with remaining pudding mixture. Garnish with remaining pineapple and additional cherries. Refrigerate until ready to serve.

Tip: Always mix brownies with a spoon. Never use an electric mixer.

Brownie Holiday Dessert

16 to 20 Servings

1 package Duncan Hines®
   Moist Deluxe Cake
   Mix (any flavor)

FROSTING
 5 cups confectioners sugar
 ¾ cup Crisco® Shortening
 ½ cup water
 ⅓ cup non-dairy powdered
   creamer
 2 teaspoons vanilla
   extract
 ½ teaspoon salt
   Red food coloring
   Chocolate kiss candies

1. Preheat oven to 350°F. Grease and flour one 8-inch round and one 8-inch square pan.

2. Prepare cake following package directions for original recipe. Pour 2 cups batter into round pan and 3 cups batter into square pan. Bake and cool cake following package directions.

3. **For frosting,** combine confectioners sugar, shortening, water, non-dairy powdered creamer, vanilla extract and salt in large bowl. Beat at medium speed with electric mixer for 3 minutes. Beat at high speed for 5 minutes. Add more confectioners sugar to thicken or more water to thin as needed. Reserve 1½ cups frosting for decorating, if desired. Tint remaining frosting pink with red food coloring.

4. Place square cake on serving platter bottom-side up. Cut round cake in half. Place each half top-side up next to square as shown. Spread pink frosting on cake. Use reserved frosting for writing Valentine greeting and decorating edges. Garnish with chocolate kiss candies.

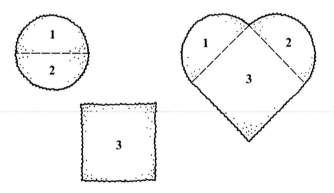

Tip: For a lovely presentation, assemble cake on large baking sheet or serving platter covered with lace doilies.

HOLIDAY FRUIT CAKE

20 to 24 Servings

1 pound diced candied
    mixed fruits
8 ounces candied cherries,
    halved
4 ounces candied
    pineapple, chopped
1½ cups chopped nuts
1 cup raisins
½ cup all-purpose flour
1 package Duncan Hines®
    Moist Deluxe Spice
    Cake Mix
1 package (4-serving size)
    vanilla instant pudding
    and pie filling mix
3 eggs
½ cup Crisco® Oil or
    Crisco® Puritan® Oil
¼ cup water
    Light corn syrup,
    heated, for garnish

1. Preheat oven to 300°F. Grease 10-inch tube pan. Line bottom with aluminum foil.

2. Reserve ¼ cup assorted candied fruits and nuts for garnish, if desired. Combine remaining candied fruits, nuts and raisins in large bowl. Toss with flour until evenly coated. Set aside.

3. Combine cake mix, pudding mix, eggs, oil and water in large bowl. Beat at medium speed with electric mixer for 3 minutes (batter will be very stiff). Stir in candied fruit mixture. Spread in pan. Bake at 300°F for 2 hours or until toothpick inserted in center comes out clean. Cool completely in pan. Invert onto serving plate. Peel off foil.

4. Brush cooled cake with hot corn syrup and decorate with reserved candied fruit pieces and nuts, if desired. To store, wrap in aluminum foil or plastic wrap, or place in an airtight container.

Tip: Store leftover candied fruits in airtight containers in freezer.

Kid Pleasers

CHOCOLATE CHIP LOLLIPOPS

2 Dozen Cookies

1 package Duncan Hines®
  Chocolate Chip
  Cookie Mix
1 egg
2 teaspoons water
  Flat ice cream sticks
  Assorted decors

1. Preheat oven to 375°F.

2. Combine cookie mix, contents of buttery flavor packet from Mix, egg and water in large bowl. Stir until thoroughly blended. Shape dough into 24 (1-inch) balls. Place balls 3 inches apart on ungreased baking sheets (see Tip). Push ice cream stick into center of each ball. Flatten dough ball with hand to form round lollipop. Decorate by pressing decors onto dough. Bake at 375°F for 8 to 9 minutes or until light golden brown. Cool 1 minute on baking sheets. Remove to cooling racks. Cool completely. Store in airtight container.

Tip: For best results, use shiny baking sheets for baking cookies. Dark baking sheets cause cookie bottoms to become too brown.

Chocolate Chip Lollipops

FOOTBALL CAKE

12 to 16 Servings

1 package Duncan Hines®
    Moist Deluxe Devil's
    Food Cake Mix

FROSTING
  ¾ cup confectioners sugar
  2 tablespoons Crisco®
    Shortening
  1 tablespoon cold water
  1 tablespoon non-dairy
    powdered creamer
  ¼ teaspoon vanilla extract
    Dash salt
  1 container (16 ounces)
    Duncan Hines®
    Chocolate Layer Cake
    Frosting

1. Preheat oven to 350°F. Grease and flour 10-inch round cake pan.

2. Prepare cake following package directions for original recipe. Bake at 350°F for 45 to 55 minutes or until toothpick inserted in center comes out clean. Cool 15 minutes in pan. Invert onto cooling rack. Cool completely. Freeze cake for ease in handling.

3. **For frosting,** combine confectioners sugar, shortening, water, non-dairy powdered creamer, vanilla extract and salt in small bowl. Beat at medium speed with electric mixer for 2 minutes. Beat at high speed for 3 minutes. Add more confectioners sugar to thicken or water to thin frosting as needed.

4. Cut frozen cake and remove 2-inch slice from center; arrange cake as shown. Spread Chocolate frosting on sides and top of cake. Place basketweave tip in pastry bag. Fill with decorator frosting. Make white frosting laces on football.

Note: Decorate serving plate with green-tinted coconut, if desired.

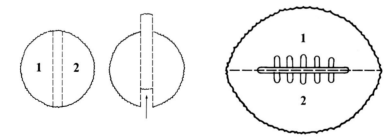

Tip: If a 10-inch round pan is not available, make 2 small football cakes by following package directions for baking with two 9-inch round cake pans. Arrange cakes as shown. Decorate as above.

Football Cake

CLOWN CUPCAKES

12 Clown Cupcakes

1 package Duncan Hines®
  Moist Deluxe Yellow
  Cake Mix
12 scoops vanilla ice cream
1 package (12) sugar ice
  cream cones
1 container (7 ounces)
  refrigerated aerosol
  whipped cream
Assorted colored decors
Assorted candies for
  eyes, nose and mouth

1. Preheat oven to 350°F. Place 2½-inch paper liners in 24 muffin cups.

2. Prepare, bake and cool cupcakes following package directions for original recipe.

3. To assemble each clown, remove paper from cupcake. Place top-side down on serving plate. Top with a scoop of ice cream. Place cone on ice cream for hat. Spray whipped cream around bottom of cupcake for collar. Spray three small dots up front of cone. Sprinkle whipped cream with assorted colored decors. Use candies to make clown's face.

> **Tip:** This recipe makes 24 cupcakes: 12 to make into clowns and 12 to freeze for later use. Cupcakes will keep frozen in airtight container for up to 6 weeks.

SURPRISE COOKIES

2 to 3 Dozen

1 package Duncan Hines®
  Golden Sugar
  Cookie Mix
1 egg
  Assorted fillings such as
  miniature gumdrops,
  candy-coated chocolate
  pieces, chocolate stars
  or whole nuts
  Confectioners sugar

1. Preheat oven to 375°F.

2. Combine cookie mix, contents of buttery flavor packet from Mix and egg in large bowl. Stir until thoroughly blended.

3. Shape thin layer of dough around desired filling. Place 2 inches apart on ungreased baking sheets. Bake at 375°F for 7 minutes or until set but not browned. Cool 1 minute on baking sheets. Remove to cooling racks. Cool completely. Dust with confectioners sugar. Store in airtight container.

> **Tip:** Stir cookie mix with fork to break up lumps before adding contents of buttery flavor packet and egg.

Clown Cupcakes

POLKA-DOT COOKIES

4 Dozen Cookies

1 package Duncan Hines®
   Moist Deluxe Yellow
   Cake Mix
¾ cup Butter Flavor
   Crisco®
2 eggs, separated
1 tablespoon milk
   Assorted colored decors

1. Preheat oven to 375°F. Grease baking sheets.

2. Combine cake mix, Butter Flavor Crisco®, egg yolks and milk in large bowl. Shape into 48 (1-inch) balls. Beat egg whites slightly in small bowl. Dip balls into egg whites. Roll in colored decors. Place 2 inches apart on baking sheets. Bake at 375°F for 8 to 10 minutes or until lightly browned. Cool 1 minute on baking sheets. Remove to cooling racks. Cool completely. Store in airtight container.

Tip: You can frost cookies with any flavor Duncan Hines® frosting instead of rolling in colored decors.

FLOWER GARDEN CAKE

16 to 20 Servings

1 package Duncan Hines®
   Moist Deluxe Yellow
   or Devil's Food
   Cake Mix
1 container (16 ounces)
   Duncan Hines®
   Vanilla Layer Cake
   Frosting
   Green food coloring
   Mini pretzels
½ teaspoon water
1 cup flaked coconut
   Narrow green ribbon
   Assorted candy suckers

1. Preheat oven to 350°F. Grease and flour 13×9×2-inch pan.

2. Prepare and bake cake following package directions for original recipe. Cool in pan 15 minutes. Invert onto cooling rack. Turn right-side up. Cool completely.

3. Tint Vanilla frosting with 3 drops green food coloring. Frost sides and top of cake. Place pretzels upright along top edge to form fence. Combine water and food coloring in small bowl. Add coconut. Toss with fork until evenly tinted. Sprinkle coconut grass over frosting inside pretzel fence. Tie ribbon bows on each candy sucker stick to form leaves. Arrange assorted sucker flowers in garden.

Tip: For a children's party, be sure to include enough candy suckers for each child.

HOT FUDGE PUDDING CAKE

12 to 16 Servings

1 package Duncan Hines®
  Moist Deluxe Devil's
  Food Cake Mix
2 eggs
1 cup water
1 cup chopped pecans
½ cup granulated sugar
½ cup firmly packed brown
  sugar
2 tablespoons
  unsweetened cocoa
1 cup boiling water
  Whipped topping, for
  garnish

1. Preheat oven to 350°F. Grease and flour 13×9×2-inch pan.

2. Combine cake mix, eggs and water in large bowl. Beat at medium speed with electric mixer for 2 minutes. Stir in pecans. Pour into pan.

3. Combine granulated sugar, brown sugar and cocoa in small bowl. Sprinkle over batter. Pour boiling water over all. Do not stir. Bake at 350°F for 45 minutes or until toothpick inserted in center halfway to bottom comes out clean. Serve warm with whipped topping.

Tip: To reheat leftovers, microwave single serving of cake on microwave-safe plate at HIGH (100% power) for 15 to 20 seconds or until warm.

BERRY BARS

1½ Dozen Bars

1 package Duncan Hines®
  Blueberry Muffin Mix
1 cup old-fashioned oats
  (not instant or
  quick-cooking)
¼ cup firmly packed brown
  sugar
¼ cup *plus* 2 tablespoons
  butter or margarine,
  softened
½ cup red raspberry jam

1. Preheat oven to 375°F. Grease 8-inch square pan.

2. Rinse blueberries from Mix with cold water and drain.

3. Combine muffin mix, oats and brown sugar in large bowl. Cut in butter using pastry blender or 2 knives; reserve 1½ cups. Press remaining crumb mixture in pan.

4. Fold blueberries into jam. Spread on top of crumb mixture. Sprinkle with reserved crumbs. Pat evenly on berry mixture. Bake at 375°F for 20 to 25 minutes or until golden. Cool completely. Cut into bars.

Tip: Blackberry jam can be substituted for the red raspberry jam.

DRUM LAYER CAKE

12 to 16 Servings

**1 package Duncan Hines®
Moist Deluxe Cake
Mix (any flavor)
2 containers (16 ounces
each) Duncan Hines®
Vanilla Layer Cake
Frosting, divided
Green food coloring
Thin pretzel sticks
Candy-coated chocolate
pieces
2 Lollipops**

1. Preheat oven to 350°F. Grease and flour two 8-inch round cake pans.

2. Prepare, bake and cool cake following package directions for original recipe.

3. To assemble, place one cake layer on serving plate. Spread with ¾ cup Vanilla frosting. Top with second cake layer. Tint 1¼ cups Vanilla frosting with green food coloring. Spread green frosting on sides of cake. Spread ¾ cup Vanilla frosting on top of cake. Arrange pretzel sticks and candy-coated chocolates on sides of cake as shown in photograph. Place lollipops on top of cake for drumsticks.

Note: For a brighter green frosting, as shown in photograph, use paste food colors available from cake decorating and specialty shops.

Tip: Spread leftover frosting between graham crackers for a delicious snack.

CHOCOLATE PEANUT BUTTER CUPCAKES

24 Cupcakes

**1 package Duncan Hines®
Moist Deluxe Cake
Mix (any chocolate
flavor)
1½ cups Jif® Peanut Butter
¾ cup chopped peanuts**

1. Preheat oven to 350°F. Place 2½-inch paper liners in 24 muffin cups.

2. Prepare, bake and cool cupcakes following package directions for original recipe.

3. Stir peanut butter to soften. Spread 1 tablespoon on top of each cupcake. Dip in chopped peanuts.

Tip: To make **Snowball Cupcakes,** frost cupcakes with Duncan Hines® Vanilla Frosting. Sprinkle with flaked coconut.

Drum Layer Cake

CINNAMON STARS

3 to 3½ Dozen Cookies

2 tablespoons sugar
¾ teaspoon ground
    cinnamon
¾ cup butter or margarine,
    softened
2 egg yolks
1 teaspoon vanilla extract
1 package Duncan Hines®
    Moist Deluxe French
    Vanilla Cake Mix

1. Preheat oven to 375°F.

2. Combine sugar and cinnamon in small bowl. Set aside.

3. Combine butter, egg yolks and vanilla extract in large bowl. Blend in cake mix gradually. Roll to ⅛-inch thickness on lightly floured surface. Cut with 2½-inch star cookie cutter. Place 2 inches apart on ungreased baking sheets. Sprinkle cookies with cinnamon-sugar mixture. Bake at 375°F for 6 to 8 minutes or until edges are light golden brown. Cool 1 minute on baking sheets. Remove to cooling racks. Cool completely. Store in airtight container.

> **Tip:** You can use your favorite cookie cutter in place of the star cookie cutter.

PECAN CRUNCHIES

3 Dozen Cookies

1 package Duncan Hines®
    Golden Sugar
    Cookie Mix
1 egg
1 tablespoon water
1½ cups crushed potato
    chips, divided (see Tip)
½ cup chopped pecans

1. Preheat oven to 375°F. Grease baking sheets lightly.

2. Combine cookie mix, contents of buttery flavor packet from Mix, egg, water, ½ cup potato chips and pecans in large bowl. Stir until thoroughly blended. Form dough into 36 (1-inch) balls. Roll in remaining 1 cup crushed potato chips. Place 2 inches apart on baking sheets. Flatten dough with fork.

3. Bake at 375°F for 8 to 10 minutes or until golden brown. Cool 1 minute on baking sheets. Remove to cooling racks. Cool completely. Store in airtight container.

> **Tip:** Place potato chips in bag and crush with rolling pin.

Cinnamon Stars

JACK-O-LANTERN CAKE

12 to 16 Servings

1 package Duncan Hines®
  Moist Deluxe Cake
  Mix (any flavor)
2 containers (16 ounces
  each) Duncan Hines®
  Vanilla Layer Cake
  Frosting, divided
  Green, red and yellow
  food coloring
1 flat bottom ice cream
  cone

1. Preheat oven to 375°F. Grease and flour 10-inch Bundt® pan.

2. Prepare, bake and cool cake following package directions for original recipe.

3. Measure ¼ cup Vanilla frosting into small bowl. Tint with green food coloring. Place ice cream cone upside down on waxed paper. Frost with green frosting. Refrigerate.

4. Tint remaining Vanilla frosting with red and yellow food coloring until frosting is desired orange color. Measure 3 tablespoons orange frosting in small bowl; add green food coloring to make brown frosting.

5. Frost cake with orange frosting. Make eyes, mouth and nose with brown frosting as desired on pumpkin. Place green frosted ice cream cone in center hole of cake for stem.

Tip: Decorate serving plate with toasted coconut mixed with green-tinted coconut, if desired.

Jack-O-Lantern Cake

SWISS CHOCOLATE CRISPIES

4 Dozen Cookies

1 package Duncan Hines®
  Moist Deluxe Swiss
  Chocolate Cake Mix
½ cup Butter Flavor
  Crisco®
½ cup butter or margarine,
  softened
2 eggs
2 tablespoons water
3 cups crisp rice cereal,
  divided

1. Combine cake mix, Butter Flavor Crisco®, butter, eggs and water in large bowl. Beat at low speed with electric mixer for 2 minutes. Fold in 1 cup cereal. Refrigerate 1 hour.

2. Crush remaining 2 cups cereal into coarse crumbs.

3. Preheat oven to 350°F. Grease baking sheets.

4. Shape dough into 48 (1-inch) balls. Roll in crushed cereal. Place 2 inches apart on baking sheets. Bake at 350°F for 11 to 13 minutes or until lightly browned. Cool 1 minute on baking sheets. Remove to cooling racks. Cool completely. Store in airtight container.

> **Tip:** For evenly baked cookies, place baking sheet in center of oven, not touching sides.

CHOCOLATE CHIP
DESSERT PIZZA

12 to 16 Servings

1 package Duncan Hines®
  Chocolate Chip
  Cookie Mix
1 egg
2 teaspoons water
2 cups miniature
  marshmallows
½ cup semi-sweet
  chocolate chips
½ cup chopped pecans

1. Preheat oven to 375°F. Grease 12-inch pizza pan.

2. Combine cookie mix, contents of buttery flavor packet from Mix, egg and water in large bowl. Stir until thoroughly blended. Spread dough evenly on pan. Bake at 375°F for 10 minutes or until lightly browned. Remove from oven. Sprinkle marshmallows, chocolate chips and pecans on baked cookie. Return to oven. Bake 5 to 7 minutes longer or until marshmallows are lightly browned. Cool completely. Cut into wedges.

> **Tip:** To cut cookie wedges easily, use a pizza cutter.

PEANUT BUTTER HANDPRINTS

About 1 Dozen Cookies

1 package Duncan Hines®
  Peanut Butter
  Cookie Mix
1 egg
1½ teaspoons water
  Assorted candies such
    as gumdrops, jelly
    beans, cinnamon
    candies and decors

1. Preheat oven to 375°F.

2. Trace child's hand on piece of paper and cut out.

3. Combine cookie mix, contents of peanut butter packet from Mix, egg and water in large bowl. Stir until thoroughly blended. Roll dough on lightly floured surface to ¼-inch thickness. Place hand pattern on dough. Cut around pattern with knife. Carefully transfer cutout cookies to ungreased baking sheets. Press assorted candies on hands. Bake at 375°F for 6 to 7 minutes or until set. Cool 1 minute on baking sheets. Remove to cooling racks. Cool completely. Store between layers of waxed paper in airtight container.

Tip: Allow your children to have fun decorating handprints with candies to form fingernails, rings and bracelets.

CHOCOLATE CHEWS

4 Dozen Cookies

1 package Duncan Hines®
  Moist Deluxe Butter
  Recipe Fudge
  Cake Mix
2½ cups frozen whipped
    topping, thawed
1 egg
  Confectioners sugar

1. Preheat oven to 350°F. Grease baking sheets.

2. Combine cake mix, whipped topping and egg in large bowl. Stir until thoroughly blended. Drop by rounded teaspoonfuls 2 inches apart onto baking sheets. Dust with confectioners sugar. Bake at 350°F for 12 to 15 minutes or until set. Cool 1 minute on baking sheets. Remove to cooling racks. Cool completely. Store in airtight container.

Tip: For **Lemon Chews** use Duncan Hines® Moist Deluxe Lemon Supreme Cake Mix.

GINGERBREAD MEN

12 to 14 Six-Inch Tall Gingerbread Men

1 package Duncan Hines®
   Moist Deluxe Spice
   Cake Mix
½ cup all-purpose flour
2 eggs
⅓ cup Crisco® Oil or
   Crisco® Puritan® Oil
⅓ cup dark molasses
2 teaspoons ground ginger
   Raisins, assorted
   candies, nonpareils or
   decors

1. Combine cake mix, flour, eggs, oil, molasses and ginger in large bowl. Stir until thoroughly blended (mixture will be soft). Refrigerate 2 hours.

2. Preheat oven to 375°F.

3. Roll dough to ¼-inch thickness on lightly floured surface. Cut with gingerbread man cookie cutter. Place cutout cookies 3 inches apart on ungreased baking sheets. Decorate as desired using raisins or candies. Bake at 375°F for 8 to 10 minutes or until edges start to brown. Remove immediately to cooling racks. Cool completely. Store in airtight container.

> **Tip:** To use as ornaments, press end of drinking straw in top of head section of cookies before baking. String ribbon through holes of cooled cookies. Tie at top.

CHOCOLATE OATMEAL WALNUT COOKIES

4½ Dozen Cookies

1 package Duncan Hines®
   Brownies Plus
   Walnuts Mix
½ teaspoon ground
   cinnamon
1 egg
⅓ cup water
⅓ cup Crisco® Oil or
   Crisco® Puritan® Oil
1¼ cups quick-cooking oats
   (not instant or
   old-fashioned)
   Confectioners sugar
   (optional)

1. Preheat oven to 350°F. Grease baking sheets.

2. Combine brownie mix and cinnamon in large bowl. Add egg, water and oil. Stir with spoon until well blended, about 50 strokes. Stir in oats and contents of nut packet from Mix. Drop by measuring tablespoonfuls 2 inches apart onto baking sheets. Bake at 350°F for 8 to 10 minutes. Cool 2 minutes on baking sheets. Remove to cooling racks. Cool completely. Dust with confectioners sugar, if desired. Store in airtight container.

> **Tip:** For a less spicy cookie, omit cinnamon.

Gingerbread Men

BASEBALL CAKE

12 to 16 Servings

1 package Duncan Hines®
   Moist Deluxe Yellow
   Cake Mix
1 container (16 ounces)
   Duncan Hines®
   Vanilla Layer Cake
   Frosting
Red licorice laces
Green tinted shredded
   coconut (see Tip),
   optional

1. Preheat oven to 350°F. Grease and flour 2½ quart ovenproof glass bowl with rounded bottom.

2. Prepare cake following package directions for original recipe. Pour into bowl. Bake 55 to 65 minutes or until toothpick inserted in center comes out clean. Cool in bowl on cooling rack 15 minutes. Invert onto cooling rack. Cool completely.

3. To assemble, place cake on serving plate. Frost with Vanilla frosting. Refer to photograph to apply licorice laces. Arrange tinted coconut around base of cake, if desired.

> **Tip:** To tint coconut, combine several drops green food coloring and ½ teaspoon water in small bowl. Add 1 cup flaked coconut. Toss with fork until evenly tinted.

CHOCOLATE PEANUT BUTTER COOKIES

3½ Dozen Cookies

1 package Duncan Hines®
   Moist Deluxe Devil's
   Food Cake Mix
¾ cup Jif® Extra Crunchy
   Peanut Butter
2 eggs
2 tablespoons milk
1 cup candy-coated peanut
   butter pieces

1. Preheat oven to 350°F. Grease baking sheets.

2. Combine cake mix, peanut butter, eggs and milk in large bowl. Beat at low speed with electric mixer until blended. Stir in peanut butter pieces.

3. Drop by slightly rounded tablespoonfuls 2 inches apart onto baking sheets. Bake at 350°F for 7 to 9 minutes or until lightly browned. Cool 2 minutes on baking sheets. Remove to cooling racks.

> **Tip:** You can use 1 cup peanut butter flavored chips in place of peanut butter pieces.

Baseball Cake

ICE CREAM COOKIE
SANDWICH

10 to 12 Servings

2 pints chocolate chip ice cream, softened
1 package Duncan Hines® Moist Deluxe Dark Dutch Fudge Cake Mix
½ cup butter or margarine, softened

1. Line bottom of 9-inch round cake pan with aluminum foil. Spread ice cream in pan. Return to freezer until firm. Run knife around edge of pan to loosen ice cream. Remove from pan. Wrap in foil and return to freezer.

2. Preheat oven to 350°F. Line bottom of two 9-inch round cake pans with aluminum foil.

3. Place cake mix in large bowl. Cut in butter until crumbs form. Place half the crumbs in each pan. Press lightly. Bake at 350°F for 15 minutes or until browned around edges; do not overbake. Cool in pans 10 minutes. Remove from pans. Remove foil from cookie layers. Cool completely.

4. To assemble, place one cookie layer on serving plate. Top with ice cream. Peel off foil. Place second cookie layer on top. Wrap in foil and freeze 2 hours. (To keep longer, store in airtight container. Let stand at room temperature for 15 minutes before cutting.) Cut into wedges.

Tip: You can use lemon sherbet and Duncan Hines® Moist Deluxe Lemon Supreme Cake Mix in place of chocolate chip ice cream and Moist Deluxe Dark Dutch Fudge Cake Mix.

BROWNIE PIZZA

12 Servings

1 package Duncan Hines®
    Brownies Plus Milk
    Chocolate Chunks
    Mix
1 egg
⅓ cup Crisco® Oil or
    Crisco® Puritan® Oil
2 tablespoons water
    Strawberry slices
    Kiwifruit wedges
    Pineapple pieces
    Vanilla ice cream
    Chocolate syrup

1. Preheat oven to 350°F. Grease 13-inch round pizza pan.

2. Combine brownie mix, egg, oil and water in large bowl. Stir with spoon until well blended, about 50 strokes. Spread in pan. Bake at 350°F for 23 to 27 minutes. Cool completely.

3. Cut into wedges; decorate with assorted fruit. Top with scoops of ice cream, then drizzle with chocolate syrup.

Tip: For convenience, purchase pre-cut fruit from the salad bar at your local grocery store.

BANANA SPLIT REFRIGERATOR CAKE

12 Servings

1 package Duncan Hines®
    Moist Deluxe Banana
    Supreme Cake Mix
1 envelope whipped
    topping mix
1 package (4-serving size)
    vanilla instant pudding
    and pie filling mix
1½ cups milk
1 teaspoon vanilla extract
6 maraschino cherries,
    drained and halved
1 ripe banana, sliced
½ cup thinly sliced fresh
    pineapple pieces
¼ cup coarsely chopped
    pecans or walnuts
½ cup hot fudge ice cream
    topping, warmed

1. Preheat oven to 350°F. Grease and flour 13×9×2-inch pan.

2. Prepare, bake and cool cake following package directions for original recipe.

3. Combine whipped topping mix, pudding mix, milk and vanilla extract in large bowl. Beat at medium speed with electric mixer until stiff. Spread over cooled cake. Place maraschino cherry halves, banana slices, pineapple pieces and pecans randomly on topping mixture. Drizzle with fudge topping. Refrigerate until ready to serve. Cut into squares.

Tip: To prevent banana slices from darkening, slice into small amount diluted lemon juice. Drain thoroughly before placing on cake.

24 Bars

BROWNIES
**1 package Duncan Hines®
Brownies Plus Peanut
Butter Mix, separated
1 egg
⅓ cup water
⅓ cup Crisco® Oil or
Crisco® Puritan® Oil**

TOPPING
**⅓ cup sugar
⅓ cup light corn syrup
Peanut butter packet
from Mix**

FROSTING
**½ cup semi-sweet
chocolate chips
2 tablespoons butter or
margarine
1 tablespoon light corn
syrup
¼ cup sliced almonds, for
garnish**

1. Preheat oven to 350°F. Grease 13×9×2-inch pan.

2. **For brownies,** combine brownie mix, egg, water and oil in large bowl. Stir with spoon until well blended, about 50 strokes. Spread in pan. Bake at 350°F for 25 to 28 minutes or until set. Cool in pan while preparing topping.

3. **For topping,** combine sugar and ⅓ cup corn syrup in heavy saucepan. Bring to a boil on moderate heat. Stir in contents of peanut butter packet from Mix. Spread over warm brownies. Cool 10 to 15 minutes.

4. **For frosting,** combine chocolate chips, butter and 1 tablespoon corn syrup in small saucepan. Cook, stirring constantly, on low heat until melted. Spread frosting over peanut butter layer. Sprinkle with almonds. Cool completely. Refrigerate until chocolate is firm, about 15 minutes. Cut into bars.

Tip: Always use the pan size called for in Duncan Hines® recipes. Using a different size pan can give bars an altogether different texture.

Candy Dandy Brownies

12 to 16 Servings

1 package Duncan Hines®
  Moist Deluxe Cake
  Mix (any flavor)

FROSTING
  1 cup semi-sweet
    chocolate chips
  5 cups confectioners sugar
  ¾ cup Crisco® Shortening
  ½ cup water
  ⅓ cup non-dairy powdered
    creamer
  2 teaspoons vanilla
    extract
  ½ teaspoon salt
    Chocolate jimmies or
      sprinkles
    Assorted decors
    Candy gumdrops
  2 maraschino cherries, for
    garnish

1. Preheat oven to 350°F. Grease and flour one 8-inch round cake pan and one 8-inch square pan.

2. Prepare cake following package directions for original recipe. Pour about 2 cups batter into round pan. Pour about 3 cups batter into square pan. Bake at 350°F for 30 to 35 minutes or until toothpick inserted in center comes out clean. Cool following package directions.

3. **For frosting,** melt chocolate chips in small saucepan over low heat. Set aside. Combine confectioners sugar, shortening, water, non-dairy powdered creamer, vanilla extract and salt in large bowl. Beat at medium speed with electric mixer for 3 minutes. Beat at high speed for 5 minutes. Add confectioners sugar to thicken or water to thin frosting as needed. Divide frosting in half. Blend melted chocolate chips into one half.

4. To assemble, cut cooled cake and arrange as shown. Frost cone with chocolate frosting, reserving ½ cup. Place writing tip in pastry bag. Fill with remaining ½ cup chocolate frosting. Pipe waffle pattern onto cones; sprinkle with chocolate jimmies. Spread white frosting on ice cream parts; decorate with assorted decors and gumdrops. Top each with maraschino cherry.

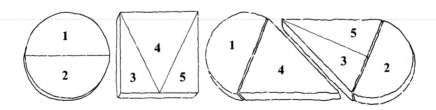

Tip: For ease in handling, freeze cake before cutting into
ice cream and cone shapes.

Ice Cream Cone Cakes

Index

RECIPE INDEX

PRODUCT INDEX